HOLLYWOOD - RED, WHITE & BLUE

HOLLYWOOD - RED, WHITE & BLUE

Roy Schreiber

With Many Thanks to:

Barry, for reminding me to say where I was going.

Jon, for gently telling me how best to get there.

Zelda, for saying okay.

Bonnie, for her kindness and information.

David, for keeping track of everyone, and I mean everyone.

Special collections staff at the UCLA library for their help with Jerry's pictures.

Contents

Preface
How Could I?

You probably noticed. Aside from the word "Hollywood," the title of this book gives very little away. Something about patriotism in Hollywood, perhaps? Perhaps. What you'll find is the biography of a family who lived in Hollywood. Most of the chapters deal with the fifteen years between 1945 and 1960. Why those years? Because that's when the world beyond our family stormed into our lives and came close to damaging each of us beyond repair. It was the era of the Red Scare. Patriotism in Hollywood was, indeed, of the super variety.

Not unexpectedly, well-known people have drawn most of the media attention as Red Scare victims. A steady stream of books and films has appeared about famous Hollywood figures who lost their jobs because of Communist Party connections, real or imagined, and about high government officials who suffered the same fate.

As you could tell from the opening paragraph, they were not alone. Because of this scare, Metro-Goldwyn-Mayer fired my uncle, who then came to live with us. That's only the start of his adventures. The FBI investigated him and the House Un-American Activities Committee forced him to testify. My immediate family soon became caught up in his misfortunes. The U.S. government fired my mother from her Air Force secretarial job. In the end, no one living in our house on Bloomfield Street in North Hollywood escaped unaffected. Even family members beyond Bloomfield street felt the impact.

So how does this make my family different from the others in Hollywood and throughout the country who became victims of that hysterical age? We're different because this ordinary family fought back and won. Out of the many thousands of people who lost their government jobs during the 1950s, only a few hundred ever got them back. My mother was one of them. And my uncle? True, he didn't return to MGM, but he had a lifelong talent for moving up in the world. Despite their best efforts, the Red-hunters couldn't keep him down.

I can guess what many of you are thinking. "Sounds like a great story, but maybe too great. How do I know this isn't a fairytale?" Good question. Even under the best of circumstances, memory is a slippery beast. Still, there's no getting around it. A great deal of what appears in this book about my family comes from what I remember. Sometimes that memory seemed crystal clear, but when I checked written records, I found it didn't happen, at least not the way I remembered it. Sometimes the memory had vanished, only to reappear unexpectedly, sparked by an incident, a snapshot, or a hidden word association. Its very reappearance caused doubt about whether it really took place, especially for events I witnessed more than a half-century ago. And in some cases, I can only present hearsay evidence, some of it thirdhand, about incidents that took place even further back than that.

With all of these obstacles, why didn't I turn this work into a piece of fiction, a novel, and leave it go at that? Here I could feed your doubts further by reminding you of one possible motivation for doing just that: memoir writing pays better than fiction. If I'd wanted to follow that path, all I had to do was write about some popular person and then squeeze myself into the picture.

How could I do that? Let's try this possibility. For many years, I lived down the street from the movie and television star Bob Hope. Not long after I first learned to drive, I almost ran him down as he walked toward the nearby town of Toluca Lake. Besides being closely identified with conservative politics, Mr. Hope was a well-known womanizer. At the time, I had a pretty teenaged girlfriend who babysat for rich people. Perhaps I actually tried to run him down because.... But no, I'll leave that kind of memoir to others.

So, why did I write the book you find here? Because I found an example of how to do it successfully. I ran across *Wild Swans*, by Jung Chung. She tells the story of three generations of her twentieth-century Chinese family. To be more specific, she tells the story of how the women of her family survived some truly awful events, and how these happenings affected her family's life. Her book acts like a camera, with both a zoom and a wide-angle lens.

It may seem odd that a book about a Chinese family would act as a model for one about an American Jewish family. I'll spare you all the bad jokes about Jews and Chinese restaurants. But in one way or another, China and the Chinese are part of my life. I have a Chinese-born wife, though to listen to her accent, New York and not China is the first place that comes to mind. It is also true that for years before I met her, since my days as a graduate student wandering the British Museum, Chinese art and culture have attracted me. They still do. As I write these words, two genuine ninth-century Tang dynasty "Fat Ladies" statues stare down at me from a nearby shelf. So it's not odd. In fact, given all those Chinese connections, *Wild Swans* as an appealing model makes sense.

Then there's my training as a professional historian. My family may not be figures from seventeenth- and eighteenth-century Great Britain about whom I've done most of my research, but the approach to researching them is largely the same.

When it comes to the similarities in research technique, however, there is one exception—the oral history. What I did for this book covered a wide and unfamiliar range. Recently I've spoken with a couple of my cousins (and confirmed through e-mail) information about family genealogy and history. But the bulk of the oral history comes from doing "silent" research in my teenaged years. Silent oral history? In those days, I rarely asked anyone a direct question. Most often I just overheard conversations when relatives traded stories. Being young, quiet, and ignorable had its advantages. Servants and quiet children are seldom noticed, and the conversation flows around them.

Another part of the information comes from working with more traditional forms of historical evidence. For instance, many families take pictures; both sides of mine did so professionally. To start with the largest collection, my uncle accumulated thirty boxes of photographs of Broadway's and Hollywood's famous and not so famous. His widow donated these pictures and negatives to the UCLA library special collections. The Pasadena Playhouse and the Huntington Library have also accumulated quite a number of his photographs. In addition, from the beginning of the twentieth century, both sides of the family saved snapshots and home movies, against which I could check my recollections and recover images long forgotten.

Over and beyond the visual materials, wherever possible, I have used the most traditional form of all, written records. Not surprisingly given his personality, my accountant father meticulously recorded and saved factual information all his life. I even have his high school report cards and yearbook as well as his college transcripts. His father, a self-educated entrepreneur, left a couple of drafts of his memoirs. He never produced a final version, but each draft revealed something new about him and his family.

Next comes my diary. Beginning in February 1957, with a one-year gap, I wrote in that diary about a page a day, nearly every day, for the next six years. I stopped writing almost exactly a month before President John Kennedy's assassination. I did not open the diary again until nearly forty years after making that last entry. Whatever my current disappointment at this stopping place, what I did find more than compensates for it.

Upon first rereading the entries, I discovered a spelling-challenged, lonely, stuck-up, know-it-all teenager obsessed with girls, grades, teachers, friends, politics, plays, and movies, more or less in that order. By the end I also found comments that still ring true about people and how they dealt with each other. I also found I had developed the ability to laugh at myself. While these firsthand observations are hardly likely to displace either Samuel Pepys or James Boswell from their literary pedestals, they do record what I did and what I thought about at the time. The diary is also on deposit with the UCLA library special collections.

Finally, as my immediate family lived its life, various government agencies tracked their activities. These agencies included the FBI and the House Un-American Activities Committee. Many of those records have survived and, thanks to the Freedom of Information Act, a fair number of copies have come my way.

Although I have altered a few names to protect those who might be sensitive, what you will find in the following pages involves real people, what happened to them, and what they did about it. Despite some twists and turns, most, but not all, of these people did manage to live happily ever after, but at times it was a near thing.

Roy Schreiber

ONE

Cast of Characters

Hoosier Hospitality

I was a long way from Hollywood when they came up out of their seats waving theirs fists and yelling at me, "No! No! No!" It seemed like a hundred of them. From the front of that high school cafeteria, with all the heavy, wooden tables pushed back against the wall, nothing stood between me and them except a microphone. As I looked, startled, at those angry faces, I didn't know their large numbers were the least of my worries. After the debate, a Republican Party operative, a chunky, Nixonian Quaker with a fringe of beard, told me that a quartet of the bigger, burlier World War II veterans sat in the front row to "shut my mouth" if I said anything "dirty" or "unpatriotic." Even without that information, I should have been frightened by their shout. But mostly, they surprised me.

In the winter of 1970, on the snowy night driving over to the little Indiana town in the next congressional district to debate its congressman about the Vietnam War, I had come up with this really clever scheme. It made no difference to me that, when I got there, I discovered the debate organizers had scheduled my opponent to speak first and last. With a scheme as clever as mine, surely speaking order wouldn't matter. Besides, word had it that the only congressional bill my opponent had ever sponsored prohibited the "spider" flag of the United Nations from ever "flying" on the moon. Based on that quality of mind, it seemed unlikely he would overwhelm the audience with his clever rejoinders to my comments.

As it turned out, he read a canned speech written by his staff. In the process, his then smiling constituents heard the win-the–Vietnam War stuff they came to hear, the stuff of God-fearing, red, white, and blue Americans.

If I had even a flicker of doubt about my ever-so-clever plan, after watching the enthusiastic audience reaction to a dull and unoriginal speech, now I knew for sure I had to use it. Some pointy-headed, commie, Jew, atheistic professor standing up and calling the war an immoral conflict wouldn't cut the path to their hearts. No, the gimmick of choice had to be much more secular, much more practical: The United States did not have an infinite amount of power; it needed to carefully select the places where it would use that power. By 1970, clearly Vietnam was not the right place. As citizens of the United States, we ran the danger of letting the communists draw us into these lush jungles where we would expend all our energy on a nation unworthy of our passion. Then, when these same communists attacked some place that really mattered, we would not have the will or the power to respond. I considered myself doubly clever because I figured none of them would get the sexual undertones.

The funny part is, as a gimmick, the argument worked just fine, at first. The people in the audience reacted as if they had never heard that approach, and all of a sudden the mold they planned to fit round the commie speaker looked like it had the wrong shape. They just sat there, puzzled, even thoughtful, trying to figure out how to react.

Smugly, I took the next step toward getting them to use their heads rather than their patriotic instincts. Two years before, Nixon went to China, but not long after a clash on the border between the then Soviet Union and "Red" China, I suggested that the United States should play the two communist powers off against each other. That's what brought them to their feet, screaming at me. They knew communism. They knew it was the universal evil, the devil come to earth. They knew the devil did not have factions or parts, and even if he did, they were not going to play with them. Most important of all, they knew all of that in their guts and reacted accordingly.

Unfortunately I discovered this information only after the debate ended, when quizzical and considerably calmer members of the audience stayed afterwards to check me out further. Still, I came away from the evening feeling that each side could boast of victories in the debate. The congressman told his audience what it wanted to hear, and I escaped without a large emergency room bill and with the tires on my nearly new Volvo unslashed. However, some days later, I did receive a pencil-written, block-printed postcard at my house.

Members of a shadowy, right-wing group calling themselves the Minute Men wanted me to know they had an eye on me.

By the time I got home late that evening, rather belatedly, I wondered whatever possessed me to think I could safely go into hostile territory like that. Did I really believe I could change anybody's mind? Well, without realizing it, in this adventure I combined two strands of my upbringing: the adventurous and the rational. These two ways of making my way in the world came from growing up in rather unusual living conditions for a middle-class Jewish family in the 1940s and 1950s. Between August 1950 and the last months of 1956, my home in California contained an extended family. It consisted of my younger brother, Barry, my father, Wilbur, and my mother, Beatrice, her brother, Jerry, and their mother, Nettie. For all intents and purposes, I grew up with two fathers and a mother-and-a-half.

So how did politics come to play a part in this somewhat unusual family arrangement? In order to understand the role politics played in this drama, first you have to get to know the actors. As it turns out yet once again, the personal is political and visa versa.

The Focused Accountant

The rational strand of my upbringing definitely came from my father, Will, as he preferred people to call him. In spite of some truly awful grades in his accounting classes at New York University, he became a bookkeeper or an accountant or sometimes a treasurer. The title depended on which firm hired him and how much they paid. Of medium height, he had black hair that started turning gray before he reached forty. For most of his life the female members of the family thought he looked skinny, and my mother and grandmother made earnest efforts to fatten him up.

In his youth, despite his modest physique, sports attracted him. Dad played both tennis and the role of an undersized lineman on his high school football team in Bloomfield, New Jersey. As it turned out, he showed some real ability in tennis. He took pride in a powerful and accurate second serve. As for football, he should have picked another sport. At some point he received a back injury that my mother claimed caused him to become sway-backed. My Uncle Jerry used to joke that someone could put a full martini glass on top of his brother-in-law's ass when he was standing up, and it wouldn't spill. Actually, after age forty or so that changed. For reasons unknown, when dad stood or walked, he developed an increasingly pronounced tilt to the left.

From what I could tell, he accepted his somewhat unusual shape with good grace, but he had another "injury" that he never managed to shrug off so casually. From his youngest days, my father had a speech hesitation. Late in his life he found an article that claimed a physical rather than a psychological defect caused the hesitation. Perhaps. Particularly when he became excited or overly anxious to make a reply, he'd fight hard to put air into his voice box. It could take him three or four tries to do it and get out the first words of a sentence. Once those first words exploded into hearing, the rest did follow without any hesitation, but he remained self-conscious about that initial pause all his life.

Texting would have thrilled him. Long before the days of voice mail, he hated answering the telephone. No matter how he handled the incessant ringing, he couldn't win. How could he ask someone else to save him the embarrassment of a phone conversation when he couldn't get the request out of his mouth? As a boy, his bar mitzvah caused him genuine agony. So did his senior speech. Unfortunately, on set occasions throughout their senior year, Bloomfield High School required all students to give one in front of the whole graduating class.

Since my brother and I grew up before the days of the home schooling movement, my father never considered preventing either of us from going to high school. But as we reached our pre-teen years, he became adamant that neither of his sons would ever "suffer" a bar mitzvah, nor the religious training that led up to it. His views on the subject made mother somewhat uncomfortable, but she did not fight her husband about one of the few family issues on which he had strong feelings.

It always seemed to me that my father's determination to go into accounting gave him a way of limiting conversation. Especially during income tax season, which lasted from January through March, he could be alone with his numbers. Without anybody questioning his reasons, he could largely avoid speaking for about a quarter of the year. Family members received the same treatment as business associates because he brought his work home for both evenings and weekends. With folders in hand, he retreated to a quiet room into which he let in virtually no natural light. Everyone knew not to disturb him. With a single, hooded desk lamp directing its light at the page before him, he wrote down what he found with great precision and clarity.

The lack of conversation had other advantages. It enabled dad to focus his attention on one problem at a time. The funny part is that he presumed everyone else operated the way he did. Once, when he was well into his eighties, he drew me aside for a private chat. We sat in the large study of his retirement community condo with its panoramic view of the coastal hills. For him there was nothing unusual in this style of conversation. If he had to talk, he preferred to do it privately on subjects he selected. In this case, what he wanted to tell me involved something that most people would consider private. Sitting in a comfortable arm chair behind his oversized desk, he said he feared that he was going senile and that my brother and I would need to take the appropriate actions to look after him and my mother. Quite naturally I asked him why he thought he had that condition. He replied, "Do you know sometimes these past few months I will walk into a room and I can't remember why I went in there?"

Holding Center Stage

If my Uncle Jerry ever detected a similar weakness in himself, he would have made a joke about it. Physically, he was about the same height as his brother-in-law, but there the resemblance ended. Although he knew he had something short of movie star good looks, he also knew how to present himself with the flair of a showman, to take advantage of what he did have. In his youth his wavy, blond hair and blue eyes gave him his two most attractive features. For the first he had expensive haircuts. For the second, fashionable clothes that brought out the blue. Even into his sixties, with his hair now cut short, he still had enough vanity to use peroxide for enhancement. As for the rest of his appearance, in spite of the fact that he chain-smoked, he always had an inclination to put on weight. Even so, he never became what one would call fat.

While my father lived into his nineties, Jerry died before he reached seventy, just like his father. I have no idea if my uncle ever thought about the possibility of a relatively early death. He certainly went through life as if he had been cast in a play, in his mind more often a satire than a drama. He behaved as if he belonged in the center of a stage, surrounded by an appreciative audience. Often, he attracted one. He had a gift for storytelling, made all the more entertaining by a bit of judicious exaggeration. His dinner-time tales covered a wide range of topics, from the people he encountered, to shows he enjoyed, to his latest sure-fire scheme to amaze the world. He had an actor's desire to draw attention to himself. More than once, just before diving into the swimming pool, I heard him say, "Okay, everybody out. I'm coming in."

Unlike my father, Jerry became a good athlete in more than one sport. While I taught myself to play tennis, Jerry taught me to swim, dive, ski, and sail. His athleticism came from a highly developed sense of space, distance, and timing. He impressed me with it in sailboat racing, when he hit the starting line in just the right place and right as the gun sounded. Behind the steering wheel of a moving car he often left me and other drivers breathless, with hearts pounding. The cops did not react well to this talent. Driving a fire-engine-red Ford convertible for most of the 1950s, he had a string of traffic tickets including, he claimed, one for failing to yield the right of way to an emergency vehicle.

My guess is that this same sense of space, distance, and timing also contributed to Jerry's artistic accomplishments. Textile design first attracted him, but he exhibited his talent most consistently in the field of photography. As a teenager living in New York City, an uncle gave him a basic Brownie camera. Early on he realized his camera could take him to places he wanted to go. During the 1930s he became a professional, working in various capacities with theater people, some of whom became quite well known. Famous or not, they always needed to have their pictures taken.

The production companies, like the Schuberts, who presented the plays also needed publicity shots for advertising. Among his earliest assignments, he photographed live action pictures of the British D'Oyly Carte Company during its New York run of Gilbert and Sullivan operettas. Those photographs subsequently became part of a book about the company that stayed in print for many years. By way of contrast, he also did publicity stills for Minsky's burlesque house.

Original Broadway plays represented the bulk of his work through the early 1940s. While serious pieces like the drama *Abe Lincoln in Illinois* starring Raymond Massey, are there, musicals occupied most of his time. Included among them is the last Rogers and Hart musical collaboration, *Pal Joey*, starring Gene Kelly.

One of the few name-dropping stories Jerry told, and one I could check from printed sources, concerned Gene Kelly in 1941. Jerry then had an apartment on West 49th Street, near Manhattan's theatre district. Returning to the city after the then traditional Broadway summer break, Kelly briefly needed a place to stay while looking for a place of his own before he once again took up his starring role in *Pal Joey*. Jerry provided it.

By 1943, my uncle moved to Hollywood where, ironically, motion picture people also had a need for still photography. His collection has over three hundred formal portraits of actors. Virtually none of them ever made it big in the movies, but they still paid him good money to take their pictures. At times he did make a good living from his profession, although he often managed to live beyond his means. When I arrived in L.A. in 1950, he owned a house in the hills above Hollywood, actually located on Hollywood Boulevard. On a clear day through the huge picture window in his living room I could see to Catalina Island, and on a clear night, with the help of a telescope, I could see the screens of many drive-in movies.

Of course by February 1951 Jerry was broke again and rather than borrow more money, he moved in with us in our new home in North Hollywood, where he became my second father.

Wanting Center Stage

On a clear day from our backyard on Bloomfield Street I could see the backside of the hills from which Jerry had just moved. Most area residents considered our current street much less fashionable than the Hollywood Hills. We now lived in a house that looked like someone had moved it from New York City. Our very un-California dwelling had been built out of cement blocks, had two stories plus a basement and sloping roof. As a gesture toward California culture, it also had a small, poorly designed swimming pool.

My mother's increasing attraction for the west coast provided the reason for our move to Los Angeles. I don't think her brother's presence "drew" her there in the usual sense of the term. Rather, I see her desire to make the move as one of several ways she paralleled her brother's instincts. They had other parallels as well. Like him, Bea (never Beatrice) had a tendency to put on weight, but she did so much more dramatically than he did. I would guess that between the time when I became conscious of such things, and her death about seventy-five years later, my mother gained and lost and gained again something over five hundred pounds. Her weight was not her most variable feature, however. Honestly, until I found some photographs of her as a girl, the natural color of her hair remained a mystery to me. Right offhand I can't think of a color she did not try at some time in her life, from raven black, to bleached blond, to old-lady blue. The length varied as much as the shade, with what effects I leave to the imagination.

Maybe these unexpected changes when she returned from the beauty parlor came from strong motivation on her part. Like her brother, she, too, needed the limelight. Whereas Jerry sought it mainly by storytelling about others, mother did it by keeping the focus much more on herself. Besides altering her physical appearance, she had other ways of attracting attention. If she did something at work that drew a compliment from a superior, she brought his flattery to the dinner table. If she had a health problem and her doctor commended her on how well she endured treatment, regardless of the body part or function involved, that likewise came to the dinner table.

My mother's egocentric behavior didn't happen without reason, and the reason goes back to early-twentieth-century American views on the appropriate role of women in society. She had rebellious ideas. She wanted to be someone special beyond her family life, but found herself blocked by traditional ideas about a woman's place. There is more than a little irony here. Both Jerry and my father unenthusiastically attended a college or university and decided to leave before receiving their degrees. They made that choice. On leaving high school, despite her good academic record and despite her burning desire to earn a college degree, my mother's parents insisted she get secretarial training instead.

In her parents' view—a largely correct one, as it turned out— one day she would become a middle-class, home-bound, Jewish mother. To fill the gap between high school graduation and marriage, she needed something practical to bring in a few dollars. A lengthy, profitless academic distraction most likely wouldn't lead to anything useful. Besides, even if they had wanted to support their daughter's academic ambitions, neither Nettie nor her husband, Barney, then had the cash to fund it. Their income grew very slowly. While Bea lived in their home, they demanded she take a job as soon as possible. She did. For more years than anyone then imagined, she worked in dull jobs in business and civil service.

It could not have pleased her that her financial contribution to her parents' household expenses freed up money for her brother's education. At least indirectly, mother helped pay for her younger brother's degreeless years at Lafayette College and Cooper's Union art school. Yes, without a doubt, my mother had her reasons to want the family to make a big deal out of whatever she did.

Given the way her parents treated her, it wouldn't have been a surprise if my mother had developed a rather negative view of her family. Yet family in the wider sense mattered a great deal to her. She knew the names of all family members including distant cousins; she even knew those still living in England. She could tell you all the details about their marriages, how many children they had, and for whom they were named.

Once in Los Angeles, she began creating a group that included both other family members and friends that mother "adopted" into the family. These Jewish women had much in common with her. Not only were they roughly her age, but also, contrary to everyone's expectations, they too had to remain employed in order to help their families maintain a middle-class standard of living. Most important of all, they had young children.

Although she would have denied it, mother competed fiercely with all of the members of her group. This sense of competition expressed itself in a variety of ways. One of them involved hosting social events that required massive amounts of food, and a guest list to match. I cannot remember more than a handful of times when fewer than twenty-five people attended one of these events, and at least once a year the number came close to one hundred. With such crowds, seating often presented a problem, and I spent my share of these get-togethers leaning against a doorway with a half-filled paper plate in one hand and a plastic fork in the other.

During these massively attended events, virtually every flat surface in the house had something edible on display. From bowls of mixed nuts and candy on the end tables, to platters of well-cooked roast beef or bowls of coleslaw on the kitchen and dining room tables, all the public space played a role in winning the competition.

Like diving or gymnastics, this competition required judges. Mother's women friends and relations played that role. They passed judgement on the quality and quantity of the food at both the beginning and end of the event. Lots at the beginning and little at the end earned the highest marks. Mountains of food that tasted "out of this world," to use one of my mother's favorite descriptions, ideally led to praise from all. Still, these women could be hard on their own performances.

"My matzah balls weren't as light as I usually make them," the maker might say, owning up to her fault. After polite protests to the contrary, the others would agree with her, sometimes just a bit too eagerly.

The presentation of the food in the dishes seldom, if ever, received a mention because any attempt at artistic arrangement seemed pretentious to them. Besides, as soon as someone took a helping, it ruined the design. More importantly, fearing leftovers, they worried that people's natural reluctance to spoil a pretty design might prevent anyone from even sampling a dish. If a dish remained untouched, the hostess received low ratings from the gathered throng of critics, regardless of the reason.

Actually, I had an experience that demonstrated their fears were most likely groundless. Some years after I left home, at the bar mitzvah of a second cousin, the catering staff produced a life-sized bas-relief of the diminutive thirteen year-old honoree, done in chopped liver. Most of the guests showed no hesitation in devouring it.

But social gatherings, to paraphrase the Gershwin lyric, are sometime things, and did not provide the main focus for competition among mother's set of women. At this point my brother and I came into play, so to speak. There is an old joke about the Jewish grandmother who takes her two grandsons shopping. In the store she runs into a friend she has not seen for some time, and the friend quite naturally comments on the grandchildren:

"Such lovely boys, how old are they?"

"The lawyer is five and the doctor is three," replies the proud grandmother.

That's the way my mother's group viewed their sons, and she believed in those goals with great passion. Unlike some of her group who had only daughters, having two sons meant that one of them could, indeed, become a lawyer and the other a doctor. She wasted no time putting her plan into operation. From the time I started the first grade, mother began telling me that I needed to get all "A"s so that I could get into a good law school.

Looking further ahead, she also wanted her sons to have Jewish wives. Each would then provide her with two grandchildren, one boy and one girl. For obvious reasons, until my teenage years, that goal didn't receive much attention. Then, when I dated a girl for the first time, mother always asked two questions:

"What's her last name?" and "Is she Jewish?"

A Hard Life

If my mother's mother, Nettie, had any goal for either her son or her daughter, I never heard her discuss it. All her life her main concern was holding her own, and doing so was always a problem for her. She became a widow in January 1944. The year after, she moved in with my parents and stayed with them until her death more than thirty years later. At least our house in Hollis, Queens, was a duplex, and so my grandmother and her youngest brother, Bob, lived in the upper half.

When we moved to North Hollywood, Nettie occupied the bedroom right next to my parents', separated only by a small, connecting closet. Jerry, my brother, and I slept in a space above them, directly underneath that slanted roof, in a large unheated and uncooled attic with two small windows, one at each end.

Nettie did not involve herself very much in rearing her grandchildren, which is why I said I had a mother-and-a-half. While she did compulsively do some house cleaning, the kitchen provided her with her primary occupation. In it she used her near dictatorial authority to relegate my mother to very defined and largely minor tasks, except when it came to the huge social events. Then, by necessity, mother achieved a more equal footing.

When we had any company for meals, but especially during many family dinners, my grandmother did not eat with everyone else. She ate earlier, alone in the kitchen. Once everyone else sat down in the dining room that overlooked the misshapen swimming pool, she considered it her duty to circulate around the table, pot or casserole dish in a heavily gloved hand, seeing to it that everyone's plate remained full until we exhausted the supply of food. She accomplished this task with great seriousness, quickly countermanding any attempt at refusing food with a rapid movement of a large serving spoon and the single word, "Eat!", spoken emphatically.

To give Nettie her due, she rarely singled out my brother and me for special attention. Also to her credit, to the best of my recollection, guilt-inducing comments about starving Chinese children never came into play when we didn't want to eat our broccoli. The fact remains, if she cooked it, we were expected to eat it, just like everyone else.

Nettie's family background accounts for much of her behavior. She started out with little. While still under five years of age, Nettie, the eldest of four sisters and three brothers, came to the United States from Budapest, Hungary, with her family, the Greenfields (Grünfelds). Reputedly the family had once lived quite nicely as estate managers for a wine-producing aristocrat. The Greenfields were not Hungarians, but German-speaking Jews. Her mother, Rose, and father, Ignatz, even spoke German, not Yiddish, to each other. To the end of her days, when my grandmother became particularly upset, she reverted to German for her swear words.

Ignatz, one of many children, may or may not have earned a good living before he immigrated to the United States. I have heard him described as a peddler and a merchant. Whatever the case, once he arrived, he earned his living as a tailor in New York. Based on what people did say about their living conditions, after immigrating to New York, my great-grandfather had a marginal income.

One undated full-length picture of him, taken by a photographer with studios at the corner of 3rd Avenue and 112th Street, shows a relatively young man with dark hair and a handlebar mustache neatly waxed with turned-up ends. He is elegantly attired in a suit with a waistcoat. The formality of the picture is enhanced by a watch chain extending from a pocket in the waistcoat, and, of course, by the white shirt and tie. He has a serious expression on his face, but he's gazing off into the distance, his mind clearly on other things besides having his picture taken. Perhaps he was thinking of how far down he had come in the world.

From what one of his sons has said, he could be a brutal man. On more than one occasion, he took a baseball bat to the unfortunate male child who had provoked his anger. I have a picture of his youngest son, Bob, as an adult kneeling by Ignatz's grave with the date of death, April 7, 1913, and his age, fifty-three, clearly visible on the tombstone. I can only wonder how much his children missed him.

While Nettie and the other girls did not suffer physical brutality, they were far from the standard picture of the Jewish American princess. Meanwhile, their mother, Rose, occupied herself with producing and nursing a child every other year for about fourteen years. Bob arrived only a couple of years before his niece, Bea. As for Nettie, being the oldest child, from an early age her parents expected her to help raise her brothers and sisters. By her teenaged years, they wanted her to work outside the home in a sweatshop.

Judging by Nettie's pictures, she looked quite attractive as a young woman: slim with darkly red hair. (Friends nicknamed her Red.) I have a picture of her as a teenager, holding baby Bob in her arms with the other solemn-looking brothers and sisters lined up in front of her. Given Nettie's living circumstances, it is hardly surprising that, at age eighteen, she married and left home.

It's difficult to imagine anyone more different from Ignatz than Nettie's happy-go-lucky Jewish English husband. True, like Nettie, Barney Robinson came from a family with numerous brothers and sisters. There the similarity ended. As a young man, Barney's parents allowed him to perform in London music halls. Some of his relatives talked about how, when in high spirits, he would jump up on the nearest elevated flat surface to sing and dance. Later in life he learned how to put a finish on pianos. No one ever said if he got his start repairing the damage his dancing had done to one of them, or if he realized he needed a steady income.

While in his twenties, whatever his profession at the time, Barney decided to seek his fortune in the gold fields of Australia. Around 1905 he signed up as a stoker on a ship that he thought was sailing in that direction. He ended up in New York instead, dead broke. Luckily, one of my grandfather's many sisters, Lena, had moved to New York a couple of years earlier. She gave Barney room and board until he found a job. As it happened, Lena worked in the same sweatshop as Nettie, and they had become best friends. After Lena introduced her best friend to her brother, the marriage followed less than a year later.

After her husband found work with the Steinway piano company, my grandmother set about raising two children of her own in the Bronx. Life may have become somewhat better for her than when she acted as a surrogate mother to six brothers and sisters, but in the first years of her marriage, financially, the difference proved very slight. In order to stay out of the real slums, she needed to work outside the home. Before World War I, American society frowned upon such behavior from a respectable, married woman. Even so, for many years, early each morning my grandmother felt she had to sneak out of the apartment to the sweatshop where she worked. The humiliation cut her deeply. Throughout Nettie's life, it seemed as though just as she thought things were looking up, they slid backwards. It made her a hard, pessimistic woman.

In other ways, besides family life, the world seemed to conspire against her. Many relatives claimed that she invented fitted sheets for beds, but that a dishonest patent attorney stole the invention and marketed it to a bedding manufacturing firm. Earlier, she and her husband scraped together enough money to buy a vacant lot in the north Bronx. Years later, when she wanted to sell it and make a profit on raising property values, surveyors discovered that bedrock lay only a couple of feet below the surface. That meant it would cost a great deal to put a house on the lot and greatly reduced its value.

These misfortunes extended to a more personal level. As long as I knew her, and I guess for much of her adult life, she really would have enjoyed drinking the occasional beer. She genuinely liked the taste. Unfortunately even a sip of anything alcoholic produced a flaming, throbbing rash on her neck that lasted for hours. When well into her sixties, at the reception when Jerry married for the second (and she hoped the last) time, the toastmaster offered the traditional champagne toast. Nettie refused to drink the champagne because of her allergic reaction. Someone (I do not remember the person's identity) with a sadistic sense of humor asked Nettie, did she want the second marriage to fail like the first one? Because, as this individual pointed out, she had not drunk to the couple's success after Jerry's first ceremony. So, reluctantly, she took that sip of champagne and waited. Nothing happened. I watched the expression on her face turn from sour apprehension to great pleasure. That is when she took another sip and within seconds the rash was back with a vengeance.

I Once heard a social worker who had prowled the immigrant slums in the early 1900s make the observation that the Gentiles drank and the Jews gambled. Nettie would not have minded doing both. Given her reaction to alcohol, however, she learned to limit her vices. She loved gambling of all kinds, but here, too, she faced misfortune. Besides one of the world's longest unlucky streaks at all games of chance, she showed no great skill at the card games that required something more than luck.

A couple of her little old lady friends in L.A. had a good deal more talent at card playing than she did. For several years, once a week, a portion of her Social Security check became theirs. From occasional comments Nettie made, I think she knew that every so often they let her win small amounts. She thought they took pity on her. I think they did it to keep her coming back to their game. To add insult to injury, because of a phone call from a mean-spirited neighbor, one afternoon the police raided this private card game. I suspect the cops had difficulty stifling their amusement at finding a room full of little old Jewish ladies in flowered dresses, looking very sheepish. They found only poker chips, no cash, on the table and so could not arrest anyone.

Perhaps the prospect of having to call home for bail money was why, from then on, my grandmother stopped playing cards with this group. Instead she saved up for the periodic bus trips to Las Vegas. Needless to say, no great or even small winnings came her way there, either, but she still went and played regularly. Evidence of her continuing enjoyment, or addiction, reached well into her eighties. Once, upon discovering that the charter bus company had cancelled the trip because their one and only bus had broken down, she refused to postpone her Las Vegas trip. For the first time in her life, she boarded an airplane and flew there.

All of these circumstances produced a woman who had very little sense of humor, who always expressed a pessimistic attitude about all things great and small, who worried about and remained extremely conscious of the monetary value of everything, and who gave affection very sparingly.

The world had not dealt kindly with Nettie, and she had her own way of dealing with these multiple misfortunes. While my parents and Jerry rarely had arguments among themselves, all three of them frequently had their differences with Nettie—loud ones, at that. My recollection is that she almost always initiated the conflict.

The way Nettie saw it, the other members of the household all too often did not measure up to her expectations. As for her now adult children, she picked at them for many years, presumably even before I saw her doing it.

"Bea," Nettie would say, "you're getting fat; you should go on a diet." Alternatively I can remember her saying, "Bea, you never eat what I cook. Look at all that good food going to waste." When it came to Jerry, his spendthrift ways presented a fair-sized target.

While she seldom, if ever, made comments about my father to his face, mother heard them often enough. So did I, when she and

Nettie talked too loudly. While living in California, it always seemed to me that the root cause of Nettie's discontent (though never said in so many words) centered on my father's failure to earn sufficient income to allow my mother to become a full-time housewife. This failing forced her daughter to work outside the home, just like Nettie had done. To my grandmother, that made all of us lower class. The Robinson family history looked like it could not stop repeating itself.

I have no doubt my father became aware of his mother-in-law's opinion of his failings. As a result, virtually the only times I ever heard my father yell involved Nettie. Over the years he became increasingly critical of both her words and behavior. While I am sure he found her low opinion of his earning capacity galling, looking back on it now, he had other reasons to shout. If I had found myself with an insomniac mother-in-law only the distance of a small closet away from my bedroom, I, too, would have done some yelling, even with a speech hesitation.

With Nettie as a model, my mother never shied away from verbal fireworks. In her view she had two sons who often proved uncooperative, unappreciative, and in need of straightening out. She showed no reluctance to say so. At times of special frustration, a smack across the face was far from an unusual event. Yet in terms of volume and frequency of her comments, neither my brother nor I ended up on the receiving end as many times as was Nettie.

In this look at my household thus far I have not mentioned politics as a subject for conflict, but it had its potential. So at this point it does seem useful to say something about where these people stood politically. Although like most Jews, my grandmother had been an FDR fan, in the presidential election of 1948, her hero having died, she probably did not vote. My father voted for Dewey, the Republican; my mother voted for Truman, the Democrat. As for my uncle, his FBI file indicates the agents watching him thought he had sympathy for the Independent Progressive Party, just like lots of other Hollywood Communist Party members, and that he voted for its candidate, Henry Wallace.

TWO
Success and Failure
Bumpy Start

Especially in the late nineteenth century, it would have been rare to find Jewish immigrants from Europe who headed directly for Hollywood. The Jews took their time. Unlike the Irish, who plunged right into politics almost immediately on reaching the United States, the Jews took their time getting involved here as well.. First they wanted to reach what they considered a comfortable, middle-class existence, and they spent at least a generation or two getting there. The Schreibers didn't strike out on some alternative path. Business, not politics, was their main concern for a very long time. The move into politics may have been slowed even further because the family did not come over in one group but rather traveled to this side of the Atlantic on many different vessels that left Europe between the late 1850s and early 1880s.

They began coming over at the end of the first wave of nineteenth-century German immigration. Adding the pejorative adjective, Jewish, to the family's German origins probably gave them the incentive to sail for New York. From what I heard, "added" is the proper way to describe what happened. A distant relative told me the family began as German Catholics who lived in Hungary, then part of the Habsburg Empire. Presumably they went to Hungary initially as part of the ruling family's effort to keep the Hungarians in their proper, subordinate place. According to this relative, a young Jewish man, escaping from Russian pogroms, fled to Hungary where the Schreibers gave him a place to stay. In the end they adopted the young man and his religion.

My guess is, given the local citizens' Roman Catholic faith and Hungarian nationality, they now felt they had a God-given right, and a patriotic duty, to give the newly minted *Jewish* German Schreibers a hard time. Faced with that pressure, gradually Schreiber after

Schreiber headed for the Lower East Side of New York City. In so far as it is possible to check these things out, a cousin of mine did go over to Hungary and discovered the burial places of many non-immigrant Schreibers in the Roman Catholic cemetery. It's only after their arrival in the United States that I can pick up the family history, beginning with my grandfather, George.

Searching through surviving snapshots and formal photographs, I found one of him as a relatively young man. He's sitting on the outside steps of a brownstone house in Newark. On his lap is my four- or five-year-old father and a younger sister. Everyone is smiling. They grin with genuine smiles, not the smiles of people told to say "cheese" by the photographer. Even in the early 1930s the photographs show the by-now-middle-aged George still looking quite handsome. In one photograph his black hair peaks out from beneath the straw boater hat with its dark band. His trim figure is well set off by his summer white linen suit and matching white shoes. And yes, he's still smiling.

George, ever smiling, ever optimistic, produced my primary source for Schreiber happenings between the 1880s and the 1940s in the form of a memoir. In it, he wrote that his father, Frank, came to New York toward the end of the Schreiber migration to the United States. Frank was born in 1858 and didn't appear on the Lower East Side until 1876. By 1881 he felt prosperous enough to marry twenty-one-year-old Henrietta Bullock, who, like her husband, possessed a rather unusual name for a German Jewish immigrant from Hungary. She was the daughter of a practicing midwife. Before her marriage, Henrietta worked as a maid for wealthy New York families, not in her mother's profession. Frank had a more typical job for the European Jewish immigrants of that era. Since he had no formal education in the United States, like so many others in his position, he made men's clothes. Between the two of them Frank and Henrietta produced twelve children including two set of twins, each set consisting of a boy and a girl. Born in 1882, George came first.

In his dozen or so typewritten pages of memoirs, my grandfather does describe a few events from his youngest years. One is the great blizzard of March 1888, in the aftermath of which he watched his father and other relatives dig out of the snow that covered their apartment house to the second floor. They all lived in the same building, and with little space and less money, they needed to buy food virtually every day, especially with young children in the house. They didn't have the luxury of waiting for the snow to melt, or the money to pay someone else to shovel it.

The other happenings George described from his single-digit years had a much more personal flavor and involved the big three: violence, sex, and race. As for the violence, not all of it was intentional. He remembered his mother screaming as she watched her year-and-a-half-old son, Leopold, fall to his death from the second floor fire escape.

Some of the violence was intentional. Not too long after Leopold died, Frank beat up a neighbor so severely that the man ended up in the hospital. As George describes the incident, the neighbor had "insulted" Henrietta. He does not explain the nature of the insult or the neighbor's connection, if any, to the other Schreibers or Bullocks.

In hopes of giving the police time to forget about what he had done to the other man, for a year Frank fled to Philadelphia along with the rest of his immediate family. Here for the first time my grandfather saw African Americans living nearby and discovered that they, too, lived like equally poor immigrant families.

Despite these occasional asides, my grandfather mostly wanted his memoirs to record his Horatio Alger–style rise in the world of business. It turns out he had good reason for his smile.

Because the family began its life on this side of the Atlantic so desperately poor, even high school was out of the question for George. After grammar school, Frank found his son a job where he worked. For what sounds like the utterly ridiculous salary of $2 per week, George began his working life by pulling the basting threads out of newly made coats. Yet shortly before the turn of the twentieth century, with the rent at $8 a month, George's salary paid for it—that is, it did so for as long as he could work. "Could work" is the key phrase. He had a seasonal job. Every summer, during the slow season, the firm laid off virtually all the workers, including both Frank and George. Only in 1901, when my grandfather reached nineteen years of age, did he find what he described as a steady job. An anti-Semitic drugstore owner in Newark, New Jersey, hired him as a "porter" for the fantastic sum of $6 per week.

Ambition and Creativity

As things turned out, from that unpromising start, he pretty much made a straight line upwards in the world. The first step came by means of a mechanical contraption he devised with his next employer, a drugstore owner with a much better attitude.

As part of George's job, he took care of the "soda fountain," where the drugstore sold soft drinks and ice cream as a side business. Before the days of refrigerated trucks, a good portion of this work involved not just selling the ice cream but also making it by means of a hand-cranked churn. My grandfather thought he was wasting time cranking, so he talked the owner into buying an old bicycle. It became the basis for a machine that used peddle power rather than arm strength to churn the ice cream.

The invention freed more than George's arms. In a modern-day gym, when people work out on a stationary bike, many of them read rather than watch television. So did my grandfather. He studied the material needed to become a pharmacist, or druggist, to use the term of his day. His dedication impressed the owner so much that he actually gave George time off to go to a local pharmacist's school in Newark. By 1904 he passed the certifying exam.

The kind-hearted drugstore owner may have been a marvelous person, but, as it turns out, he came up somewhat short on business skills. Two years after my grandfather earned his pharmacist's license, this very nice man discovered he had bought at least one too many drugstores and could not pay his bills. By now George managed the store where he worked and made almost $20 per week. The owner offered to sell it to him for $500 down and $50 per month for the balance. In spite of the fact that the down payment represented nearly six months salary, my grandfather accepted the offer. At age twenty-four, with a minimum of formal education, he had entered the capitalist class.

Finding the Cutting Edge

I don't know what it is about photography that draws in members of my family, but it most certainly does. I do know that George's attraction had nothing to do with it as an art form, but rather as a business venture.

In 1905 the film business had just begun. Notice that I said film, not photography. In the 1880s, Kodak's founder, George Eastman, sold a camera using glass plates to capture images. It cost $50. By the turn of the last century, thanks to Kodak, rolls of film replaced glass plates inside cameras. With the new film came the

Brownie camera, and by 1900, just about any middle-class family could afford one. Kodak sold 100,000 of them in the first year.

These days what we loosely call drugstores sell, in addition to medicine, just about any portable item. They also provide at least one service virtually everyone can name: They reproduce photographs. It's easy to forget that these links between drugstores and photography had to start some place.

Back in the 1880s, after taking the pictures, Kodak had its customers send the camera containing the exposed film to its factory. The slogan "You press the button, we do the rest." sounds lovely, but it masks substantial delays in getting back both the snapshots and the fully reloaded camera. People began to explore alternatives, but finding a convenient place to develop pictures could easily turn into something of a treasure hunt. Realizing the problem, Kodak then tried a do-it-yourself developing kit, but that device never really attracted large numbers of amateur photographers. In 1905, after five years of affordable photography, the sales of cameras had outpaced the processing locations.

To get in on this camera boom, once George owned the drugstore in Newark, he approached Kodak about selling their cameras and film. Even more innovatively than this new way of getting customers into the store, he stumbled on the idea of installing a film-developing lab right in the back room. He told me that he had most of the chemicals he needed to develop film already on hand. At first my grandfather's friends asked him if he would do them a favor and develop a few roles. Eventually the word got around, and he saw the business possibilities. Through articles in magazines meant for druggists, he then publicized what he did nationwide.

Before World War I, he established a business that did nothing but develop film and called it Sterling Photo Finishing. He sent messengers to drugstores to bring back the undeveloped film and a week later had them return the developed snapshots or slides. From that point on, innovations just kept rolling out. In his memoir, George lists all of them he can remember, but one particularly impressed me. He employed and trained blind people to work in the darkrooms of his developing plants. Notice the plural. By the 1940s he had established a plant in lower Manhattan as well as the one in New Jersey.

As my grandfather moved up in the world, he brought his extended family with him. One of his plants had spare space on the ground floor, and there he installed his father in his own tailoring shop. His brothers and brothers-in-law gradually joined him as equal partners in Sterling Photo Finishing. As a result, they all became quite comfortable and ultimately some of them or their progeny became millionaires.

Not long after my grandfather bought that drugstore in 1905, he married Esther Weiss. I have a copy of their wedding invitation for the ceremony and reception at the Lenox Assembly Hall at 252 Second Street in New York. The invitation gives all of the necessary information in both German and English. As you might have guessed, Esther Weiss and her family were also German Jews who came from Hungary. A cousin of theirs, Eric, made something of a reputation after he started calling himself Harry Houdini. She and George first met each other as children when they both lived on the Lower East Side.

Although my memory of Esther is not very vivid, I do recall her as small and rather thin. She looked like she took the world a lot more seriously than her husband did. She had the reputation for being as bright as George, and one of her daughters characterized her as a woman of strong family loyalty and considerable determination.

The earliest pictures that I've seen of Esther come from around 1910. They show a woman dressed all in black, wearing a matching, wide-brimmed hat with artificial flowers of the same color on top. In most of the pictures, the hat acts as a kind of veil in reverse. Only her nose and mouth show, so it's difficult to get a full impression of her appearance.

One picture, however, reveals her whole face. In this three-inch-by-two-inch snapshot, I can see the shadow of a man in a derby who took the picture. In it, Esther is standing in front of a brownstone house, most likely the one in Newark in which she and George lived. That huge hat is pulled back, revealing an attractive, narrow face with a nose that is just a bit too big for it. At first sight, her long-sleeved dress looks quite modest, but it has a plunging neckline. Only a thin necklace covers a tiny portion of her bare skin. She must have been proud of that necklace to show it off that way, because it looks like the weather has turned cold. George stands facing her in his overcoat and homburg hat. They both have that smile.

My guess is that necklace is an indication that George and Esther were beginning their climb to prosperity. Once the money started flowing in, they moved from Newark to Bloomfield, New Jersey. They remained there until the last of their three surviving children married and moved away, and then they took an apartment in Asbury Park near the beach.

So far in the Schreiber saga it is mostly a tale of triumph after triumph, and to the end of his life George remained an optimist in whom creative juices continued to flow. Yet the phrase I mentioned earlier, "surviving children," indicates that they did not totally escape misfortune. Their youngest daughter, born in 1916, lived only two years and died of diphtheria.

I also had the impression that sometime during the 1920s George and Esther's marriage became strained. In her pictures from this era, Esther's smile looked like an effort, something she preferred not to do. Her lips appear thin and pressed tightly together. It is difficult to know if it was the cause or the result of this strain, but another woman appeared on the scene. Her name was Florence, and she worked in the New Jersey photo finishing plant. The mutual attraction between George and her caused many complications and produced some unpredictable results.

Among their other problems, Florence was considerably younger than my grandfather. With the big spread in their ages, over twenty years, they needed some plausible reason to spend time together outside of work. So Florence found ways to occasionally date my father.

Now I know that these days the term "date" can have a variety of meanings, but no one ever even hinted to me that in this case it meant anything more than my father and Florence saw each other socially. According to dad, the first time he ever went up in an airplane, in the late 1920s, some barnstorming pilot came in a biplane to an airport near Bloomfield, and my father took Florence flying in it.

This effort by George and Florence to hide the relationship evidently did not fool the family forever. The relatives/partners in Sterling Photo took George aside and told him that Florence had to go, both from his life and from the plant. They did succeed in getting her fired, but just how successful they were in getting her out of my grandfather's life remains something of a question. In 1963, after a long illness, Esther died. The following year my grandfather secretly married Florence. She had remained single all that time.

By the time they married, Florence no longer worked as an employee of a photo finishing firm. She owned a gift shop at Newark Airport, and though not as wealthy as George, money certainly did not worry her. I saw her collection of Asian-style furniture, with its dark wood and intricate design, and it must have cost quite a good deal. I have a suspicion that at least some of the money for the shop came from my grandfather.

He claimed that they planned to start by spending weekends together to see if they were compatible enough to live with each other full time. Even at their age, maybe because of their age, the values of respectable nineteenth-century America stuck with them. Swinging Sixties or not, they could not bring themselves to live together even part of the time without getting married first. Yet they knew that in the end they might have to get divorced. By keeping their relationship quiet, they thought if a divorce proved necessary, none of their friends and relations would have to find out.

I also wondered if the family's earlier reaction to their relationship might not have had something to do with their efforts at secrecy. Even if they stayed together, George and Florence might have feared conflict with family more than they feared the embarrassment of publically ending the marriage.

Although George and Florence clearly knew within a year or two that they could live amicably, they went on with their secretive arrangement. Doing so proved awkward in many ways. My grandfather had to dream up a whole series of excuses why he couldn't see his family on the weekends. After he gave me a particularly vague one, I asked my aunt, with whom I was staying temporarily, what was going on. She replied with a laugh that if she did not know better, she would swear that her father was keeping a woman some place.

Then, in 1967, Florence had a heart attack. It forced her to sell the gift shop and move to George's Asbury Park apartment. Once again he needed to care for a seriously ill wife. Florence survived until 1969. The following year, at age eighty-eight, my grandfather announced to me: "I'm through with marrying women, They still keep chasing me, but I couldn't take another one getting sick and having to look after her." Ever the optimist, the reverse situation never occurred to him—that he could have a long illness and his wife would look after him. It turned out he had good instincts. Three years later, in 1973, he died after a brief illness.

A Long Shadow

As I mentioned before, my father told me the story about dating Florence and the airplane flight, and without realizing it, he framed the chief problem of his life. Even under the best of circumstances, it's not easy having a brilliantly successful father and then finding an independent path away from him.

Given what dad did well and given his handicaps, he had it rougher than many others in his position. It is difficult to imagine any area in which he could shine to the extent his father did in so many. Certainly not sports: football brought him a bad back and tennis provided no real audience. On the personal side, it could not have done his self-image any good to discover that a woman he dated really wanted to get close to his father. Not surprisingly, the editors of his high school yearbook noted dad's excessive shyness in the caption under his picture. What's more, when it came to a career path, he could see the fate that most likely awaited him. As they came of age, virtually all of his first cousins went to work at Sterling. Here, once again, dad could find himself eternally on display as the kid who never could reach his old man's level.

In 1927 this looming fate most likely caused dad to leave NYU without a degree and take a job with a firm of accountants in Newark. A year later, he switched to Sears, Roebuck, where his salary went from $5 to $15 a week. He may or may not have known that was less than his father had earned at the same age.

Finding success often has a lot to do with good timing and good luck. My father throughout his life had very little of either. Two years after he quit school, the stock market crashed, the Depression rolled over everyone, and lots of people were thrown out of work. Uncharacteristically, here dad proved more fortunate than many. Unemployment only caught up with him in June 1934, and then only briefly. By August he took a job as a bookkeeper with a furniture firm.

In 1934, after four years of Depression, many people began to feel optimistic again. By then the New Deal legislation and President Roosevelt had raised people's spirits. Looking back from this distance, the suspicion is this attitude contained a good deal of wishful thinking. Now we know that the economic impact of the Depression lasted until World War II broke out. Yet the reality made little difference. From what parents of various friends have said, many of them chose 1934 as a year to get married. So did my mother and father on March 10 in New York City's Hotel Croydon.

They had an unlikely courtship. To begin at the most basic level, Will lived in Bloomfield, New Jersey, and Bea lived in the

Bronx, New York. Keep in mind that the 1930s came well before the era of cell phones and e-mail. What is more, virtually everyone in the middle class considered the cost of a long-distance phone call a big expense. On top of that, the state of public and private transportation in the greater New York area then (or now, for that matter) made face-to-face dating of any description rather awkward, but obviously not impossible.

When I asked my parents how they got together in the first place, they said their mothers knew one another from their years on the Lower East Side and arranged for their children to meet. Even across class lines, the Hungarian German Jewish connection evidently still meant something, perhaps especially in the marriage mart.

Yet it is not right to exaggerate the spread in their income levels too much. The Depression did not spread itself evenly, and at least some people associated with the entertainment industry in various forms could do rather well. By the mid-1930s, with two adult children paying their own way, even a piano finisher managed to put some money aside and bring in a living wage and a bit more. Barney and Nettie paid for a wedding with over fifty guests at a posh hotel.

I still have the pictures of the grand social event, both the photographs and the movies. Two things impress me: how small my father looked in comparison to my mother, and how flamboyant Jerry looked with his flowing blond hair, mustache, top hat, white tie and tails.

No, I didn't forget. Most people don't marry just to please their families. Emotions, hopefully including love, are usually involved. While as far as I know my father did not have someone in his life before he started seeing my mother, my mother had Miron. Ever since she graduated high school, she had Miron. Jerry described him as a great bear of a man, well over six feet tall. I saw his signature scrawled at the very bottom of a page in my mother's high school yearbook. He wrote that if anybody loved her more than he did, he should sign his name underneath.

Sounds promising, so what was the problem between them? Why didn't mother marry her high school sweetheart? No one ever told me. It looks as if even taking into consideration the hard economy of the times, their relationship went on like most mildly pleasant habits, because it was habitual. As 1933 ended, mother turned twenty-six, even by Depression era standards, no longer young. When my father appeared on the scene, he looked like a man with prospects, and more importantly he proposed marriage.

Did they have a great love affair that swept them both away? All I can say is, if so, in their later life the signs of this passion had vanished. As a teenager, I only saw them hold hands once. Anything other than a kiss on the cheek had to be stage-managed by others. Yet something held them together beyond inertia. They seldom exchanged hostile words, and despite my father's conversational handicap, they often talked with each other, even during tax season. In these conversations I never saw them trying to set traps for one another the way people who have unspoken hatred for each other do in a bad marriage. They stayed married for over sixty years and died within a year of one another.

After his marriage, my father's efforts to remain independent of his father and Sterling Photo continued. Beginning in 1935, for a year and a half, he tried running and owning a retail store that sold peanuts, cashews, and other basically frivolous food items to the citizens of Hackensack, New Jersey. His efforts produced a hernia, from moving around one-hundred-pound bags of salt, and a FOR SALE sign in the front window.

During World War II, dad remained a civilian. But his medical problems and becoming a father with my appearance in 1941 played no role here. He worked as an account in a war-related firm called the Elastic Stop Nut Corporation, and that kept him draft exempt.

He stayed with that firm until 1946 when he gave up his bid for independence and finally went to work for Sterling Photo. He became a vice-president of Sterling and the general manager of their Manhattan plant. Why the change? By that year he had a wife, a newborn baby, and a five-year- old son. Maybe he now felt the need of a secure, dependable job.

To make the commute to Manhattan easier, we moved from a rented apartment on Isabella Avenue in Newark to our own duplex on Francis Lewis Boulevard in Hollis, Queens. Here I traded in my New Jersey accent for a New York one.

Like I said, my father had the worst sense of timing. He took the job at Sterling when George and his brothers and brothers-in-law increasingly disagreed about how to run the firm. Even in his sixties, George wanted innovation and expansion. As they aged and worried about the fate of their adult sons, now associated with the firm as well, the other partners wanted a more conservative approach.

The disagreement lasted several years, but in 1949 they forced my grandfather off the governing board, gave him stock, a pension, and sent him to a comfortable retirement. Or so they thought. Soon after leaving, he began working on the invention of a camera that could hold two different kinds of film at the same time.

At its first opportunity, the new management of Sterling Photo sold the Manhattan plant to another firm. The new owners had no use for my father. In March 1950, at age forty-three, he found himself unemployed once again. It wouldn't be the last time.

With misfortune comes opportunity, at any rate that's how my mother saw it. For some time she had had her eye on California, but she wouldn't move there without first checking it out. So, in 1944, along with my immediate family, Nettie, and her sister, Bell, all of us took the train out to Los Angeles. Mother liked what she saw of the constant sunshine and the glamorous people. Of equal importance, the number of her family out there continued to build. Jerry and his wife, Mildred, had gone out in 1943. Around that time Nettie's brother, Murray, and his wife, Pearl, also moved to Los Angeles. These connections reinforced each other because the families really had double ties. Pearl and Mildred were sisters.

As long as dad was connected with Sterling Photo, the California move remained out of the question. But, now that link had evaporated. My mother began by talking my father into going out to Los Angeles to see what job prospects it had to offer, to see if he could make a living out there. Dad joined Jerry in the Hollywood Boulevard house and tried his hand at taking wedding and bar mitzvah pictures, using Jerry's developing lab for his work to cut expenses.

When dad left, he gave mother power of attorney over all matters back home. She used it to sell the house. According to my father's sister, mother did not tell dad about her plan until she had a buyer for the house. With final papers in hand, mother shipped everything to Los Angeles. Then she piled my brother and me into a 1940 Dodge and headed across the country with Nettie's former housemate and brother, Bob, acting as driver. He, too, planned to settle in L.A. Esther never forgave her daughter-in-law for that move.

THREE

Reds in the Blue

Exploring Leftward

Over half a century later, it's difficult to overestimate the glamor associated with Hollywood in the 1930s and 1940s. Before the days of independent productions and filming on location in any town, state, or country that offered a tax break, Hollywood was very much the center of everything connected with the movies. As far as entertainment went, the movies had a much wider national reach than Broadway. Broadway shows did have touring companies that went to major cities, but a town had to be microscopically small not to have a movie theater. Listening to songs from Broadway musicals over the radio did not offeranything like the aura attached to seeing a movie. Hollywood's drawing power existed well before the days of DVDs and downloads. Having a connection, any connection, to one of the movie studios meant seeing people on a daily basis that the rest of the nation only fantasized about seeing in person maybe once in their lifetime.

By the time World War II ended, Jerry became one of the envied. He worked for MGM. There Judy Garland and Gene Kelly, among others, sang and danced for vast sums of money, money beyond nearly everyone else's most fantastic dreams. But not Jerry's. In those days, given a choice, he preferred being a rich communist to being a poor one.

Because Jerry went to the then eternally blue skies of Hollywood in 1943 and stayed involved in left-wing political causes, I know a good deal about him. I can reconstruct a large slice of his life by following him through the pages of FBI files. Not only was there a file dedicated to him, but he also made appearances in other people's and organization's files as well. That is because he was not just a so-called fellow traveler, but a card-carrying member of the Communist

Party. In the view of FBI director J. Edgar Hoover and his allies, this membership made Jerry and his associates a threat to the American way of life, at least as Hoover and company understood it.

In a sense, J. Edgar had it right. During the Great Depression of the early 1930s (certainly while the other Hoover was president), it looked like the capitalist system in the United States, and maybe the whole world, no longer worked. As a result, the victims of the Depression often felt that only extreme solutions would improve their lives. For a number of them, the Fascists and the Nazis had the answers to restoring order and prosperity. At the other extreme, for those who wanted to combine equality with their order, they discovered the teachings of Karl Marx. The Communist Party proclaimed that people the world over should take only their fair share from society, and that all citizens should have their needs equally satisfied. Especially after the greedy commercialism of the 1920s led to the Depression, a very large number of U.S. citizens found the argument for more equality convincing.

For American Jews, so often treated as outsiders and undesirables, equality had its attractions. Looking back from the twenty-first century, it's easy to forget how socially acceptable anti-Semitism had been in the United States. Well before the 1930s (and for more than a decade afterwards), Jews could not live in certain neighborhoods, join various clubs, or go to many of the most prestigious colleges and universities.

Under these circumstances, it would have been amazing if the politics of the radical left had not attracted Jerry and many others with his background. They belonged to the second and even third generation of largely secular American Jews. By the 1920s, in spite of the anti-Semitism from sources as diverse as Henry Ford and the Ku Klux Klan, Jews had begun to move up in society. Then the Depression sent many of them back down the economic ladder. Even so, full-fledged communism gave some of them pause. The Soviet Union and Joseph Stalin as the means of eliminating injustices made them uneasy, and they looked for other models.

Many of them found one in the Republic of Spain. What other government could brag about an artist such as Pablo Picasso acting as one of its ministers? What other government had tried harder to correct centuries of social injustice? Unfortunately in the 1930s, thanks primarily to the ruthlessness of General Francisco Franco, the Republic lasted for only a short time.

When Franco and his fascist-style Phalangist Party raised a revolt against the leftist republican government, it outraged and frightened communists, socialists, and liberals all through Europe and the United States. Those feelings intensified as both Hitler and Mussolini began to aid Franco with money, weapons, and military personnel. The Spanish Republic's supporters, including Joseph Stalin, then somewhat belatedly attempted to do the same for the republican or Loyalist cause. These efforts included the Abraham Lincoln Brigade of U.S. volunteer soldiers.

By 1939, Franco won and went on to rule Spain for over thirty years. About the only remaining echos of the political left's unsuccessful efforts to block him is a well-known novel by Ernest Hemingway, *For Whom the Bell Tolls,* and the even better known painting by Picasso, "Guernica."

Less well remembered than this small number of memorable art works, the armed struggle also produced a large number of refugees. Starting in the late 1930s, they poured into France with little more than what they could carry, and in dire need of help.

This is where Jerry makes his first appearance on the political scene. He became interested and active in what became known as the Joint Anti-Fascist Refugee Committee. The committee not only recruited members from New York City, but also attracted people from all over the country who wanted to help cause of fighting worldwide fascism. They ranged from Quakers to such well-known communists as the author Howard Fast. As the committee's name indicates, several groups got together to form it, including The American Committee to Save Refugees, and the United American Spanish Aid Committee.

Although the FBI watched their actions carefully from the earliest days, the Joint Anti-Fascist Refugee Committee's members denied wanting to become politically involved. They claimed that fund-raising for refugees' medical aid occupied all their time. The Roosevelt administration, taking them at their word, provided a U.S. government license for this group to raise funds and even granted it a tax exemption as a charitable organization.

The committee may have given Jerry his start in leftist politics, but it was not his end point. The Communist Party was. Tracing the path of Jerry's involvement with the party leads down three possible paths. One looks obvious; another starts with Jerry's wife; and the last originates in his relationship with Gene Kelly and his friends. The obvious connection is most likely a dead end.

Starting in 1930, a group of left-leaning and communist photographers in New York City formed a group called The Workers' Film and Photo League. Unfortunately no membership lists survive, but based on those who publicly associated with the League, Jews represented a good proportion of their membership. They wanted to train amateur photographers, and they also encouraged professional work for exhibition or publication.

Although the League looks promising as Jerry's beginning point to party membership, for several reasons, it is an unlikely one. First of all, nowhere in Jerry's extensive FBI file is any connection mentioned with either the Worker's Film and Photo League or its successor group, the Photo League. As a rule, if the FBI could link someone "of interest" to a leftist group, they did.

Over and beyond the evidence in the surveillance files, the purpose of the Photo League and Jerry's photographic interests didn't coincide. League members devoted their energies to photographing the evils of Depression-era, capitalist America. Their subjects wandered the streets or slept in them. Photographing Gilbert and Sullivan operettas, where Jerry's career began, isn't what the League photographers had in mind.

True, Jerry did do some urban photography. Like the father figure of twentieth-century American artistic photography, Alfred Stieglitz, he frequently photographed structures such as bridges and buildings without anyone in the shot. The buildings and structures Jerry photographed came out sleek and modern, like Rockefeller Center, not like the ruins of capitalism favored by Photo League photographers. When Jerry did photograph people, they often appeared to jump for joy. This is a far cry from the Depression-haunted men and women who appeared in communist propaganda pictures of 1930s America.

So if the Photo League did not lead Jerry to the left, what did? One of Nettie's brothers-in-law, Lew, suggested the next possibility. He suggested it early and often. Over the years, Lew became increasingly bitter about the path his nephew's life had taken. Perhaps that is because they had much in common. When it came to artistic tastes and talent, Lew had a flare for showmanship. I remember his smile and the way his eyes twinkled when he laughed. Like many of his contemporaries, he sported a bristling mustache that somehow made him look vaguely comic. As for the rest of his hair, there was none. He adored cooking in the Italian style and generally kept up a fast-paced commentary on what he was doing for anyone who wandered into the kitchen. He often did so with an ersatz Italian accent that today would be considered rather politically incorrect.

As for musical tastes, Gilbert and Sullivan stood at the center of his record collection. When D'Oyly Carte came to New York during the early 1930s to produce their shows, I believe Lew did some backstage work for them. He certainly knew many of their performers. Most likely Lew recommended his nephew, the one to whom he had given that Brownie camera, as company photographer during their New York run.

When it came to their politics, Lew and Jerry once again had much in common, but what matters here is what separated them. Lew proudly and often spoke of his socialist principles. Notice the term is *socialist*, not communist. He had a visceral dislike of anything that smacked of a Soviet connection. On the subject of his once-favored nephew's political sins he said, "That woman brought the malignancy into our family."

He had in mind Jerry's first wife, Mildred. Granted, she was an interesting choice for Jerry. She came from a well-to-do and fairly large Russian Jewish family. When they first met, Mildred's brothers and sisters ranged from adults to very young children. Physically, Mildred was the only woman in her family who never weighed over two hundred pounds. Even at a young age, she did not lack magnetic qualities. One of Charlie Chaplin's sons chased her for years. Perhaps her attractiveness had something to do with her eyes, which had an almost Asian aspect to them. Mildred's long, dark brown or black hair added to the impression. In the 1940s she had two ways of styling it: Rosalind Russell's model, piled fashionably high on her head; or Veronica Lake's, worn down in a much more alluring fashion. And as long as I am using Hollywood stars of the era as examples, I should finish by saying that when Mildred spoke, she sounded a bit like Lauren Bacall.

She and Jerry started her relationship around 1939. True to their leftist beliefs, they did so without benefit of clergy. With some wry embarrassment, Mildred told one of her nieces that, despite her leftist politics and social views, she couldn't bring herself to buy a diaphragm until after their marriage. In the end, they did get married, by a rabbi. A year later they moved to Los Angeles.

As for which one of them had the lead in their relationship, my guess is that at the earliest stages, Jerry did. Mildred was a dozen years younger. She told me that, until Jerry came into her life, she had never even seen a play. Jerry's political views had already formed when they met. A small indicator in their direction comes from one of the photograph albums that Jerry put together between the late 1920s and the mid 1930s. He did the captions for the pictures, and under the one of him looking like the stereotype of a wild-eyed fanatic, he wrote, "the Communist."

Once Mildred became involved with Jerry's world, she rushed in with great enthusiasm. Most likely Lew interpreted Mildred's zeal as influencing Jerry when in fact it was the other way around. It sounds very much like Gene Kelly and the relationship he had with his much younger wife, Betsy Blair.

That brings up the third explanation for Jerry's politics, Gene Kelly. Given the offer of a temporary place to stay, the two of them must have had some form of friendship. One of Jerry's pictures from *Pal Joey* shows Kelly reading a newspaper with a headline about Franco meeting Hitler. With their politics, the shot could have been a private joke between them. Although it is true that Kelly's wife, Betsy, tried (and failed) to join the Communist Party, I don't believe Kelly, personally, drew Jerry into the party, because there is no evidence Kelly ever joined.

Jerry's connection with Kelly reflects the broader group to which they both belonged. And many of these people were communists. A spot called Bergen's on 45th Street provided a leftist meeting ground for many of them. A bar that served some food rather than a restaurant that served drinks, Bergen's was located not too far from Times Square and from Jerry's apartment. This bar became a magnet for left-wing intellectuals, where the Spanish Civil War and the finer points of Karl Marx could produce a lively discussion, if not an intense argument. Bergen's brought in just the type of people Jerry and Mildred adored. When they did join the Communist Party, they joined a trendy branch of it called the Cultural Section. Here we have many of Bergen's patrons under another name.

After December 7, 1941, it became much more difficult to maintain this type of casual lifestyle. With the outbreak of World War II, Jerry became eligible to serve in the military. Although his asthma kept him from a prime IA classification, as early as the summer of 1942, he began taking a series of defense jobs in various shipyards in the greater New York City area. Like my father's case, this sort of work meant the armed forces would not draft him.

When Jerry and Mildred moved to Los Angeles in November 1943, he found another shipyard job as a pipefitter. By April 1944, he worked his way back into the photographic field with a job that involved taking pictures of defense plants. The pressure to find young men for the service must have eased that year, because in July Columbia Pictures hired Jerry as a chemical mixer in their photographic lab.

By 1945 Jerry began taking still pictures for MGM. While just about all the Hollywood studios employed their fair share of Communist Party members and sympathizers, MGM had quite a collection of them, especially among their writers. I have no way of knowing if Jerry worked there because of party connections, but whatever his motives for taking the job, he would have considered these like-minded workmates a plus, and their presence must have helped him feel at home. Like him, many of them originally came from New York City.

As for his on-set photographic work, unlike the printed movie posters, the public then and now rarely treasured it. Whereas the posters have become great collector's items, the still photographers and their work have never attracted much attention. Yet from the 1920s onward the people who ran the movie studios recognized their value. Studio owner Jesse Lasky told his directors that selling the film had equal importance with making it, and that well-shot still photographs played a key role in that process. Along with the posters, local movie theaters displayed these stills to help lure audiences. Until I moved to L.A., I thought those stills were individual frames from the motion pictures. Perhaps the studios meant to give that impression.

Jerry made his contribution with photographs taken during the filming of such movies as *The Green Years,* an Academy Award winner. Yet the evidence indicates that this assignment, and presumably many others as well, were not solo efforts. Jerry worked alongside several other still photographers. Besides taking the publicity stills, he also took pictures of the actors as they finished for the day. These pictures helped insure continuity across many days of shooting.

The number of photographers available meant that employment at the studio was not constant. That is why, along with the work for MGM, the publicity firm of Hilman, Shane and Breyer employed Jerry to take pictures of motion picture celebrities. Looking through the ones in the UCLA collection, there is a series that included a shot of Gene Kelly, his wife, Betsy Blair, and John Garfield. Also included here are photos of Charlie Chaplin and his last wife, Oona. Given the left-wing politics of all of these people, perhaps he photographed them at an event in support of the Joint Anti-Fascist Refugee Committee. From Jerry's point of view, they paid him for work that ran parallel to his ideals.

On reaching L.A., Jerry did not revert to the position of a mere sympathizer. Both he and Mildred transferred their Communist Party memberships. At first his belonged to the Northwest section of the party, where Jerry associated himself with became known as the "writers" branch. By 1945, with a reorganization of the party groups, he ended up in something called the Hollywood-Miscellaneous section.

This Hollywood, rather than L.A., designation indicates Jerry's studio connections. In the New York area, the Broadway people mixed with ordinary citizens in party groups or "cells." On the West Coast, the Hollywood movie employees formed a separate organization that reported directly to national party headquarters. Its members did not appear at rallies under the Communist Party banner, but rather under that of sympathetic organizations. Perhaps this policy explains why Jerry remained quite active in the Joint Anti-Fascist Refugee Committee. Not too long after moving to Hollywood, it looks like he became even more heavily identified with this organization. The leftist newspaper *People's World*, in their September 29, 1944, edition, reported that Jerry had taken over the management of their Hollywood office.

As far as I can tell, running the Hollywood office sounds a whole lot more impressive than the actual accomplishments of this branch. FBI observations, or rather lack of observations, prompt this last statement. After the single mention of the post, Jerry's file never brought up the topic again. Of course, for whatever reasons, I might not have gotten all the information. However, this impression is reinforced by FBI observations of someone who was a good deal more vital to the national Communist Party than Jerry.

The person is John Howard Lawson. No doubt reflecting the innate anti-Semitism of their boss, the FBI agents observing him noted more than once that he was born Jacob Levy. This gentleman worked as a screenwriter by trade and was a devoted communist by inclination. So much so that he provided a good deal of the energy and leadership for the Hollywood group. His high position led the FBI agents who watched him to monitor his mail. Their reports list a wide variety of people who corresponded with him regularly as belonging to communist front organizations, including the *People's World*. After Jerry took over as its secretary, the agents reported only one letter from the Joint Anti-Fascist Refugee Committee to Lawson. Then there is a two-year gap to September 1947 before Lawson participates in an event sponsored by the committee. The New York, not the Hollywood, branch of the organization put it on. It hardly sounds like the Hollywood office overflowed with communist-related activity while Jerry was in charge.

Even if his position looks like more show than substance, with this level of prominence came social obligations. So the Robinson house in the Hollywood Hills on Beachwood Drive became the site of social gatherings ranging from intimate dinners to much larger events. The latter included fund-raising for various causes, such as efforts to block anti-communist legislation in Congress.

While other entertainment industry communists such as Meta Reis Rosenberg (producer of the 1950s television show *Maverick*) lived on the same street as Jerry and Mildred, not every neighbor proved sympathetic to having a steady stream of leftists at the Robinson household. That meant all of this activity did not pass unnoticed by the people who lived in the surrounding houses. My favorite observation on these gatherings comes from an FBI interview with one of their neighbors, who:

> desires to make no comments concerning the loyalty of [the Robinsons] but believes that it is questionable. Mr. [?] stated that any reason he may have to question the loyalty of the [Robinsons] is not based upon fact and arises only through suspicion such as they had parties and gatherings at their home and strange music was played at these parties and gatherings. Mr. [?] stated that it was strange in that it did not sound like American music. Mr.[?] could not state what kind of music it was…

Looking at these get-togethers from the inside, the view is somewhat different. While music may have had its place, discussion provided the main purpose for the people being there. During at least one of these gatherings, they focused on a semi-public letter written by Jacque Duclos, a French communist. In it he expressed his none too favorable opinion of the U.S. Communist Party. The Frenchman argued that the U.S. party had become so middle-class in its composition that it could hardly fit the description of the workers' party Karl Marx had in mind. Viewing the situation in Hollywood, particularly the Jews in Hollywood, Duclos knew the territory.

Although Mildred and Jerry are exceptions, judging by FBI files and testimony before the House Un-American Activities Committee, regardless of their religious backgrounds, the most active members of the party and their sympathizers often had college degrees. At this time, fewer than half the people in the United States graduated from high school, never mind college. In the case of many of those associated with the motion picture industry, they also did very nicely financially. A large number of the leftist writers, directors, actors, and technicians made salaries that qualified them as middle-class, even upper middle-class. What the average factory worker of the era made in a year, these people made in a month or less.

As a variety of both friendly and hostile observers noted, "small minority" is not the term that best describes the Jews among the movie industry's new rich. Their sizeable numbers carried over into left-wing politics. When the FBI did a demographic breakdown of the membership of the Hollywood Communist Party in February 1944, out of 319 members, they identified 200 as Jewish.

Sorcerer's Apprentice

This concentration drew the attention of a wide variety of anti-Semites. One of the best-known outbursts from this quarter came from Mississippi Democratic congressman John Rankin. He publically went through a long list of Hollywood actors, including Danny Kaye and Edward G. Robinson, and, after giving their original Jewish names, proceeded to condemn their communist sympathies. In 1945 Rankin introduced the motion in Congress that resulted in the House Un-American Activities Committee becoming a standing congressional committee with a permanent budgetary appropriation. It looked like the FBI now had institutional competition in hunting down communists. As you'll see, in Jerry's case, the competition produced a tie.

Whether J. Edgar Hoover was as anti-Semitic as Rankin is a matter of debate, but in reading about him it is rather amusing to discover that he and Jacque Duclos pretty much agreed on the situation inside the U.S. Communist Party. I would be hard-pressed to decide who hated the American Communists more, the Frenchman, because they were condescending members of the middle-class, or the FBI director, because they were uppity sons and daughters of immigrants who aspired beyond their natural, lowly place in U.S. society.

In Hoover's case, as a man for whom favorable publicity and secret information-gathering became art forms, he feared that communists would use Hollywood movies to spread their left-wing propaganda to an unsophisticated and unsuspecting American public. During World War II, he had the added frustration that the Roosevelt administration wanted to build support for its alliance with the Soviets by using Hollywood's help.

With victory against the Nazis still in doubt, the government pressed Jerry's friend, the screenwriter Howard Koch, who had won an Oscar for *Casablanca,* to do a script for a movie called *Mission to Moscow.* Hoover's letters on the subject show he did not approve, to put it no stronger than that. He called portions of the movie "a prostitution of historical fact." I have a vision of him, his misshapen mouth unconsciously twisted into a snarl, writing this commentary.

Whatever his wartime frustrations, the FBI director did have permission to keep watch on any group that he thought potentially subversive or threatening to U.S. security. That is why even during the war, FBI agents watched Jerry and Mildred and many others, and why informants reported on them from within the Communist Party. While this project kept literally thousands of agents busy, it did not necessarily lead to any kind of legal prosecution or to other unpleasant consequences for those communists under observation.

The lack of consequences did not satisfy Hoover. So, even as the war against the Nazis and their allies began, he asked his men to compile a list of left-leaning subversives. The list became known as the Security Index. Hoover wanted those listed to be treated like the West Coast Japanese Americans after the attack on Pearl Harbor. That is to say, he wanted the President of the United States to declare a national emergency, order a roundup of these disloyal Americans, and have them sent to detention camps until the emergency ended. Presumably the end would come with the collapse of the Soviet Union.

On January 2, 1945, the Special Agent in Charge of the Los Angeles Office of the FBI sent Jerry's name to the Washington, D.C., head office for inclusion on the Security Index. On January 30, Hoover signed the official letter designating Jerome S. Robinson, native-born communist, of North Beachwood Drive, Los Angeles, California, as an addition to the Index.

Fortunately the Security Index never did what Hoover wanted it to do. The question is, why? For starters, the nature of the bureaucratic process within this organization pivoted around the director's ever whim. Everyone knew about the FBI office in Butte, Montana, where unpopular and inefficient agents finished out their careers. If Hoover wanted the names of subversives, his agents saw to it that he got them. The various FBI offices around the country poured thousands of people's names into headquarters for inclusion on the Index.

As a result of this deluge of names, it became impossible to round up all of these "subversives" in any reasonable amount of time. So headquarters tried to have the field offices prune their lists. By November 1948 the Los Angeles office of the FBI received a form letter signed by Hoover concerning Jerry. It stated that his file had been inactive for some time, and unless activity took place, they should remove his name from the Security Index. In spite of these efforts at restricting the number of people added to the list, it continued to grow like cherry blossoms in springtime. Between 1950 and 1954, the list expanded from 12,000 to 26,000 names. By 1960, 430,000 files had blossomed.

The final blow to activating the Index came from the office of the president. Despite the increasing fear of communism, Hoover found he could never convince either Presidents Truman or Eisenhower to declare a national emergency. Therefore, no communist ever went to a detention camp. Not that the director stopped trying. With Hoover's firm endorsement, in 1950 Congress somewhat belatedly passed the Internal Security Act, which established the camps in which to imprison those listed on the Security Index. The act spread these camps across the country, from Pennsylvania to California. Significantly for Hoover's unfulfilled hopes, the bill passed over Truman's veto.

Yet what other practical alternative did the FBI director have? Whatever the disadvantages of pulling off a mass roundup all at once, they were nothing compared to launching individual prosecutions against everyone listed on the Security Index, even the reduced list. True, legislation generally known as the Smith Act made it a federal crime to preach or advocate the overthrow of the United States government by force or violence. In the late 1940s, the national leaders of the Communist Party did go to jail as a result of Smith Act convictions, but only the leaders. If all of the thousands of individuals under FBI surveillance had Smith Act charges filed against them, the federal courts would never see an end to the prosecutions.

Just as important, as their ability to listen to and record private conversations became more and more sophisticated, the FBI agents' ability to gather information about these people mushroomed dramatically. Often neither the field offices nor headquarters bothered to obtain the court-ordered warrants needed to make the evidence gathered by the new techniques admissible in a trial. Even with legal warrants, given all the suspects, agents would have had to spend months of their time doing nothing else but testifying. They had almost created a civil disobedience campaign in reverse. Only this time, law enforcement officers would have produced the overwhelming number of protesters that clogged up the legal system. Hoover needed some way, outside the courts and the camps, of punishing communists.

Paying the Price

As if in answer to Hoover's prayers, the House Un-American Activities Committee blundered onto the scene. As the postwar fear of the Soviet Union increased, the focus shifted more and more to the operations of the Communist Party in the United States. Various observant members of the House of Representatives and the Senate realized that hunting subversives had potential—not to make the United States safer, but to build their political careers.

The thought was hardly a new one. As World War II approached, Congressman Martin Deis, chair of a temporary version of the House Un-American Activities Committee, tried to act upon it. In the process he aroused Hoover's jealousy. As a result, Deis found nothing but hostility from all of those in the FBI he contacted.

In 1946 and 1947, the permanent incarnation of the House Un-American Activities Committee decided to focus more of its attention on Hollywood. The motivation is obvious. At this time, no one outside of Congress knew most of the committee members' names. Granted, at least one, Richard Nixon, did go on to reach a certain level of prominence, but not until after 1946. Bringing movie stars as well as directors, producers, and writers before the committee would instantly fix the attention deficit problem.

Yet promising as these prospects sound, the committee faced major difficulties. For openers, it did not have either the staff or the time to build up the necessary information to use against its hostile witnesses in the proposed public hearings. J. Edgar Hoover, however, had both, and unlike during the Deis years, now he could control all of the material.

One obstacle existed to this alliance. It was illegal. As part of the executive branch of government located in the Justice Department, the FBI reported to the president through the attorney general. None of its files should have gone to a congressional committee without the permission of the agency's superiors. President Truman had no interest in providing that permission. When rumors circulated that FBI files went to the committee, the assistant to the attorney general called Hoover to account. Hoover denied the charge. Of course Hoover was misleading his superiors. His personal files, rather than official ones, provided much of the information. He found other ways around that prohibition. Among other techniques, former FBI people worked for the committee and saw to it that its staff secretly received the confidential information Hoover thought they should have. This technique and others also enabled Hoover to direct the committee's attention in the places he wanted it to go.

For some time Hollywood films and the people who made them had Hoover on the alert. FBI files contained many reports and memorandums about movies and the messages they conveyed to the people who saw them. In some cases the production of a movie involved known "subversives," like Howard Koch. Therefore Hoover and his associates presumed communist propaganda lay buried in any plot such people devised, if the agents could only find it. Take Rick, for example, the character Humphrey Bogart played in *Casablanca*. He fought for the Loyalist side in the Spanish Civil Wars. Once again, a Hollywood writer had made a communist the hero. Case proven.

Sometimes the situation became reversed, and the movie had obvious propaganda value for the communist cause because it did things like attack racial inequality or big business. Then the FBI started investigating the people associated with making the movie to see which ones had communist connections. Since many of those who worked in Hollywood participated in fund-raising for a variety of causes and groups, including the Joint Anti-Fascist Refugee Committee, they found themselves suspect.

With considerable fanfare, the committee's Hollywood hearings (actually held in Washington, D.C.) took place in October 1947. In the end the new chair of the committee, J. Parnell Thomas, called only a small faction of the scheduled witnesses, and he stopped the hearings before the month had quite ended.

Thomas's actions threw everyone off stride. Both those of the right and those of the left came away convinced the hearings seriously injured their cause. Once again Hoover fumed about Congressional incompetence. All that work, all that effort to expose and bring to an end communist influence in the motion pictures, and it produced nothing of significance except some contempt citations. These citations went out to a group that became known as the Hollywood Ten, Howard Lawson among them. That limited impact frustrated the FBI director, and he did not forgive easily.

Not too many years later, in 1949, Congressman Thomas ended up in a federal prison, convicted of financial misdeeds. There he found a couple of members of the Hollywood Ten serving out their sentences for contempt. The thought has certainly crossed my mind that the FBI director had a hand in all of their fates. Like the Stephen Sondheim lyric says, after living through J. Edgar Hoover, everything else is laugh.

On the other side of the equation, not long after the hearings ended in 1947, those who made the decisions in Hollywood met at the Waldorf Astoria hotel in New York. Many of them, like producer Dore Schary, who shortly thereafter went on to run MGM, considered themselves on the political left. Nonetheless, however reluctantly, their final statement in essence said that they would not permit communist subversives to have employment in the movie industry. As a result, the Hollywood studios fired a wide variety of people. The notorious Black List, the one all of the studio executives at the time denied ever existed, came into existence.

Hollywood had caught patriotic fever of this type before. During World War I, Cecil B. DeMille, among others, acted as a volunteer in the American Protective League and investigated his employees when he felt they acted "un-American." He then sent the information to the Justice Department's Intelligence Office, an early version of the FBI. Thirty years later, little by little, those suspected of subversive behavior found themselves unemployed. Their number included some with high salaries and big reputations like Howard Koch. Their number also included some of much more modest means and reputation, such as Jerry. By the time I arrived in Los Angeles in August 1950, Jerry had not worked in the studios for nearly two years. What is more, he and Mildred had divorced.

Good-bye to All That

The two of them may have been politically and sexually a model couple, but in other ways they had begun to drift apart. Mildred wanted children, and Jerry did not. After some years of lobbying, Jerry agreed to become a father, but Mildred had a miscarriage. She badly wanted to try for a baby again; he did not.

Then there was money. While the two of them lived well, they always lived on the edge. For most of his life, Jerry spent money much more rapidly than he made it. When Jerry lost his job at MGM in 1947, they moved out of the Beachwood Drive house and in with Mildred's parents. Granted, they bought the Hollywood Boulevard house not too long afterwards, but the boom and bust pattern showed no signs of ending. My teenaged diary shows that as late as 1956 even I loaned Jerry the equivalent of $1,500 in today's money. Mildred did not like living that way. Finding her husband blacklisted and unemployed could not have helped.

Then along came Milton, the musician. Recognized as one of Hollywood's most talented musicians, he belonged to that elite group of performers who constantly had recording dates and supplemented them with television shows and movies. No band claimed him permanently, but he made the rounds and did very well financially in the process. Of equal importance, it looked like his success would last.

While after the divorce, neither Jerry nor Mildred altered their political beliefs, both of them virtually retired from active involvement in politics. Yet it almost seemed as if Duclos had them in mind when he wrote his letter about American communists. Money and class status mattered a great deal to them. Communism for them meant leveling upwards in society, not down. They wanted a fair system so that they could live the good life. If they could not find it together, they would find it with others.

Mildred had a good start. After a couple of failed pregnancies, she and Milton adopted one child and not long afterwards had one of their own. I visited their house often while the children were young and found a spacious but sparsely furnished California ranch-style home. The living room sofa and many chairs had stain-resistant, dark-colored, nogahyde upholstery. Unlike my parent's home, no vase or candy dish graced end tables, because they had none. Come nighttime, wall switches turned on overhead lights, not lamps. Mildred and Milton did not want to say "no" to their children any more than necessary, so they felt that the absence of breakable and stainable objects made that goal easier to achieve. A first-class swimming pool in the backyard gave the only indication that they had real money. Their eldest boy learned how to swim in it before he reached age two.

As for their relationship beyond the children, Milton never made a public complaint that I ever heard. Privately, the story may have been different. My first high school girlfriend, Catherine, acted as their live-in babysitter during the summer of 1956. While living there she found, filled out, one of those magazine surveys that ask about the quality of home life. The last question wanted sexual satisfaction rated, and a big NO appeared in the neighboring space. Who filled out the form? Well, Mildred and Milton had separate bedrooms, and only Mildred's could be locked.

Given the intertwining of the two families, after the divorce Jerry and Mildred encountered each other on at least a semi-regular basis for the rest of Jerry's life. I can remember one time when Mildred, with a baby in tow, visited Jerry at his summer rental house near the bay on Balboa Island. After calling out a greeting, Mildred came in. She found Jerry, wearing his bathing suit, laying on the living room floor and listening to music. She walked right up to him, placed her infant son on Jerry's chest, and then both of them smiled. Whenever I saw them together, they showed this easy familiarity, as if they shared a secret.

FOUR

The Wild Blue Yonder

Difficult Adjustment

Joining Jerry and dad and then settling into the good life in California proved more difficult than my mother had imagined. All of us had problems adjusting to our new surroundings, and I had about as many as anyone. Basically I repeated an earlier pattern of the New Jersey to New York move. But it seemed much rougher this time.

Granted, my first week in the Hollis I had been mugged for my Halloween candy. Even so, over four years later, I had worked my way up to where I became part of the fourth grade "in" group. Before leaving New York, not only did I have a set of three older boy friends living on the same block who treated me as an equal, but I also had my first successful encounter with a girl. When a girl named Sheila asked me, in front of witnesses, if I liked her, I replied, "You bet I do." In return she gave me a shy smile. That is as close to going steady as a fourth grader got in those days, and the prestige it earned with peers was no small matter. Even my mother's long-range plans for her future lawyer began to fall into place as well. P.S. 134 promoted me from the mid-level fourth grade class to the fifth grade class with the brightest students in it.

Lastly, before departing from New York, I began working on my allotted fifteen minutes of fame when the local newspaper, *The Long Island Daily Press*, published a picture of me participating in a play done by the neighborhood children's theater program. Granted, I wore what looks like a dress, but in fact the play took place in ancient Greece, and so technically I appeared in period costume. My role as Pocahontas in a subsequent production, in which I did indeed wear a dress, left no surviving photographs and never made the papers.

In Los Angeles, I had to start all over again. Right from the beginning, three things made the climb difficult. First came my accent. I had a New York accent with a bit of a New Jersey underlay. My California classmates quite naturally referred to me as the New Yorker. Thinking back on it, they didn't mean the term as a major slur, but it certainly made me feel singled out for the wrong reasons and encouraged me to lose that accent quickly. By the time I reached seventh grade, the verbal evidence of my New York background had almost completely vanished. It is true, however, that the accent returned when I became very tired, and that tiredness coincided with one of those rare occasions when I had to tell someone I liked to sip cidah through a stwah.

Fitting in also required the visuals to go along with the verbal, and here I needed my mother's cooperation. Every school has a uniform, whether it is called one or not. In the New York City schools during the late 1940s the accepted dress for boys included a white shirt, tie, slacks, and "good" shoes. I only wore jeans, a t-shirt, and "sneakers" after I came home from school to play with my friends and then, often under protest. I hated changing clothes in the middle of the day.

For L.A. school kids, the problem didn't exist. Given the nearly constant sunshine, students in the Los Angeles school system spent a good deal more time outside at play than I had experienced in Hollis. Jeans and sneakers made sense all day long. But not to my mother. She would not permit me to go into a classroom looking like a "ragamuffin." Once I arrived at school, I did manage to remove the tie, but the rest of the uniform singled me out as someone different from the other boys. Inside every child lives an anarchist and a fascist fighting one another. When it comes to styles of dress, the fascist wins almost every time. Not until high school did I manage to merge with the teenage herd, at least as far as my clothing went.

My formal dress style pointed toward trouble in the other place that mattered, the playground. In L.A., students played organized games of all sorts as a part of the school day. In New York City the games weren't organized. Having joined the fifth grade in what seemed to me like a foreign country, the games proved as foreign as everything else. Even leaving to one side my marginal physical abilities, every one of the students in L.A. had four years more practice than I had. So, predictably, I was lousy at games, especially anything involving a ball. This lack of ability meant that, when my fellow students chose team members, they almost always chose me last or next to last. To her credit, the fifth grade teacher at the Gardner Street School, the one nearest my Hollywood Boulevard home, noticed the difficulty. To get around it, she made me and another student of similar ineptness the team captains who selected the others.

That way of doing things took some of the edge off the humiliation, but my obvious lack of skills went too deep to totally avoid the consequences. For besides lacking the physical ability in everything from softball to touch football to dodge ball, I also lacked the vocabulary of sport. The term "heads up" gave me continual problems. One day when someone shouted those words in my direction, instinctively I put my head up and got hit with a football. If they meant duck, why didn't they just say so?

Some of this transition might have worked out more smoothly if my teacher at Rio Vista, my new school in North Hollywood, had been as sharp as the first one, but she was not. I don't know what her problem was. Perhaps she was a frustrated, aging athlete. Looking up at her from my four foot, six inch height, she looked tall and muscular, as though once upon a time she might have competed in something. By the time I encountered her, her black hair showed signs of losing its fight with the gray. That was the least of her problems. Further subtle signs of deterioration went beyond the physical.

We did assignments that she periodically wrote on the blackboard, while she spent large portions of her day singing to the class and strumming an auto-harp. I will grant that, to my recollection, the woman had a pleasant voice, for all the difference that made. Besides making it difficult to concentrate, the singing showed an indifference to her students' education. We were just so many acoustic tiles. On the other hand, distancing herself from us had its advantages, because when she did become actively involved with the students, her judgement often proved suspect.

When I first appeared in the classroom, she assigned a boy named Jimmy to show me the way things worked. This short, beefy kid developed the habit of periodically whacking me when we went out of public view. Presumably he meant this treatment to emphasize his message on the way he wanted things to work.

As for the teacher's more general problems, here is the example that stuck with me. She heard a student make offhand comment about why this individual felt disliked. To disprove the statement, the teacher told all of us to fill out what she called a "hate list." On this sheet we had to write down the name of the person in the class we disliked the most and the reasons for the dislike. This woman masquerading as a teacher then read the reasons out loud. With great self-satisfaction she indicated to us that most of the comments centered on just a couple of students, and the student who felt disliked was not one of them.

While it probably would have come as a shock to her, when the members of the class heard the "why," we knew exactly who fit the description. Just in case any doubt remained, after class I heard a few of the girls talking, and they named names, including mine. Fortunately, since we moved to North Hollywood in the middle of the school year, I only had to experience this clueless musician for less than six months.

The sixth grade teacher looked like my previous teacher's physical opposite—so overweight that the principal gave her a classroom on the ground floor because she could not get up a flight of stairs to where the other sixth grade classes were located. After graduating, I heard rumors about her anti-Semitism. She certainly had conservative political views. In April 1951, she convinced the other teachers to bring their students to an assembly. There we heard a live radio broadcast of General Douglas MacArthur's famous farewell speech, the "old soldiers never die" address that he made after Truman fired him as commander of United Nations troops during the Korean War. Still, whatever her prejudices and political persuasion, the sixth grade teacher always treated me rather well, a lot better than the auto-harp lady.

Money, Money, Money

My parents paid little attention to my efforts to fit in. They had difficulties of their own, mainly financial ones. My father's efforts at big event photography never brought in enough money to make a living. We spent 1950 mostly using up savings from New York. For a private photography business such as his to succeed, he either needed word of mouth advertising or a business manager who took care of searching out clients. While dad did good work, he did not have the kind of outgoing personality needed to stimulate one person telling another about its quality. True to form, he spoke to his customers as little as possible. A business manager would have required a percentage of the take, a set fee, or maybe both. As my father saw it, such an arrangement was self-defeating in terms of making a living wage. So in April 1951 he went back to accounting and began working for a firm that made automobile license plate frames.

In many respects it was a terrible job. The man who owned and managed the factory had a personality that might have worked in sales, the place where he started, but he proved much less effective in management. This new boss loved to exaggerate, to put it as positively as possible. What was worse from dad's point of view, he had an illogical mind. Last but not least, he cut every financial corner so tightly that ultimately he had to face charges of income tax evasion. As if all of this wasn't bad enough, dad's boss also loved to argue with his employees. When dad infrequently spoke at the dinner table, his conversation often involved the latest outrage this man committed. As if all of these horror stories dad brought home weren't bad enough, his salary totaled one-third less than he had earned at Sterling Photo.

To make up the difference, the household needed more income, and that meant relying on the other adults. Nettie contributed to the cooking, not the cash flow. Besides, I don't believe my mother could have brought herself to charge her mother rent. Jerry did put some money toward food and utilities; he contributed to the so-called house money, kept in a kitchen drawer. But he gave only a relatively small amount and frequently announced he needed to borrow from the fund. In any case, taking his well-known spending habits into consideration, his contributions may not have been as regular as my parents had hoped.

This left my mother as the last potential wage earner. During the 1920s and 1930s, besides helping in the Hackensack nut shop, she had worked both in private industry as secretary in a bank and for the U.S. government bureau that collected taxes on alcoholic beverages. By 1952 she began looking for another job and found one with a manufacturing firm, but she stayed there less than a year. Her rapid departure had nothing to do with the firm itself, but rather because she preferred a U.S. government civil service job.

Today, when "bureaucrat" is a term of abuse, that may seem an odd choice, but given the uncertainties experienced by all those who lived through the Depression, it did not seem an unusual one to them. Besides, Jews, and increasingly other minorities, felt they received fair treatment in the civil service. Before the days of civil rights legislation, that built-in fairness made a big difference. Granted, private industry provided a better salary, but in mother's view a generous retirement scheme, regular pay raises, and opportunities to advance in status, gave government work the edge. Most important of all, after the probationary period ended, the U.S. civil service provided secure employment. Mother had served her probation back in the 1930s. In October 1952 she rejoined the government civil service as a secretary for the Western Air Procurement District of the Air Force. Her pay almost exactly made up for the difference between my father's current salary and what he had made at Sterling.

Unpleasant Surprise

One catch came with these arrangements. In order to do the job, mother needed to have security clearance. Especially with the Korean War still in progress, the possibility existed that spies might want to know what the Air Force bought and where the purchases went. Getting clearance meant FBI agents would now investigate mother and everyone associated with her to see if she had any subversive connections. Actually, even if the job had been in something much more benign, like the tax unit she left years before, the FBI still would have looked into her background. These were paranoid times all over the United States, not just in little towns in rural Indiana.

Looking back on mother's government job application, one question very quickly enters my head: With a member of the Communist Party living in the house, with Aunt Pearl and Uncle Murray living nearby and active in the movement to save the convicted atomic spies Julius and Ethyl Rosenberg from the electric chair, with a full-scale war going on against the communists in Korea and one heating up in Indo-China, with the House Un-American Activities Committee and Senator Joseph McCarthy prowling about, why didn't someone living in our house figure out that a government job came with major problems?

I suppose it's fair to let my mother off the hook. In many ways she provided a model for the ideal disinterested civil servant. She never exhibited any great degree of political sophistication. Beyond family interactions, politics on any level in the wider world always remained slightly outside her field of vision. She read the newspaper, listened to the news on the radio, but up to the time her job was threatened, I never heard her make any political comments. The one remark from this period I can recall was directed at me, probably after some wise crack on my part: "This is the greatest country in the world, and don't you forget it."

Even Nettie was more likely to say something about political affairs than her daughter, though her occasional comments often had a kind of apocalyptic ring to them: "They're going to drop the Bomb; I just know it."

As for my father, he too kept up with what was happening in the world. Still, as a voting Republican, the idea that anyone would suspect him or his wife of disloyalty never had any reality to him, until it happened.

That leaves Jerry to sound a warning. He probably guessed the FBI had a file on him; after all, he had lost his job at the movie studios because of Communist Party membership; he knew people like Howard Koch and Charlie Chaplin had to leave the United States because of left-wing sympathies held by them and their wives. Why didn't Jerry warn his sister? Well, maybe he did, but fairly obviously she ignored the warning.

Once the FBI began their investigation, it quickly became a two-pronged operation. The first involved finding out mother's personal political beliefs. They checked out her attitudes by questioning relatives, friends, and neighbors going back at least ten years.

At one point they thought they had found something to use against her. When dad worked for the Elastic Stop Nut Company in 1943, the company transferred him to Cincinnati, Ohio. Someone with a similar name to mother's had signed a Communist Party–sponsored petition in Cleveland, Ohio. Since Cleveland and Cincinnati are some distance apart, even the agent in charge of the investigation wondered whether or not they had the right person. Further investigation showed that besides the problematic geographical distance, the petition had circulated two years before my parents left New Jersey.

After interviews with people on both the East and West Coasts and several points in between, no one ever remembered my mother saying anything disloyal about the United States, or anything that would indicate she might be a security risk.

As it turned out, with recently elected President Eisenhower's Executive Order 10450, the question of security rather than of loyalty now mattered most. A government employee could swear loyalty oaths on a daily basis and pledge allegiance to the flag every morning in front of a full chapter of the American Legion and the Daughters of the American Revolution but still end up with a security risk classification and no job. This is where the other prong of the investigation comes into view.

Jerry's career quickly fills up his sister's file with damning material. Much of the information I have about him from this period comes from my mother's file, not his. Amazingly, although the FBI agents obviously felt mother looked like a security risk and reached that conclusion by April 1953, she kept her job and her provisional security clearance for some months.

In spite of her questionable status, during this limbo period, the Air Force transferred her from one office to another. The first office lost personnel because of a lack of funds, but, potential security risk or not, she had enough seniority from her earlier government work to bump a more junior person out of the way. Only a month before her suspension took place, she received a glowing letter of commendation from the chief civilian administrative officer in her Air Force procurement division. This misleadingly positive state of affairs lasted until November 1953, at which point the Air Force suspended her without pay and, a year later, finally dismissed her. The proverbial bolt from the blue pretty well describes her reaction to the suspension and dismissal.

Yet some loopholes existed, making it possible to avoid the full force of a dismissal for security reasons. One way to mitigate the situation involved resigning before the completion of the loyalty investigation and civil service ruling. That way, when applying for the next job in the private sector, a person could mask the reasons for losing the government job. Pay, working conditions, difficult bosses, anything but questionable loyalty, became the stated reasons for these people's resignations. Potential employers rarely questioned such explanations.

Mother would not do that. Both my parents felt she had done nothing wrong, and to them resignation meant a back-handed admission that she had. So they decided to appeal her dismissal through administrative channels in the Air Force. The price for this stand on principle proved high. Besides legal fees, with this mark of disloyalty on her record, mother stayed unemployed for the next two years, and our standard of living declined.

Even leaving J. Edgar Hoover to one side, the anti-communist movement focused a good deal of its attention on punishing its targets. Inflicting financial hardship provides a tried and true method of punishment. At first I was only dimly aware of the financial impact on the family. Twelve-year-olds are seldom budget conscious. They know what they want, but seldom what it costs. To her credit, one time after I asked for something the family couldn't afford, mother sat down with me and went over the expenses of the household and its income. There was a gap.

Mother's experience by no means proved unique. Having a close relative who either was currently, or once upon a time had been a communist, meant government employees in the thousands either resigned or had their employment terminated. George Clooney's movie *Good Night and Good Luck*, about Edward R. Murrow, looks at just such a case that involved the Air Force as well as other similarities to mother's predicament.

An overreaction to the unseen dangers of the times is a fair statement of what happened. After all, during the early 1950s, we fought a war against the communists with guns and bombs. Giving particularly intense scrutiny to government employees with left-wing connections of any description seemed a necessary precaution in order to protect the nation from subversion. But like so many other American trends, enthusiasm overcame common sense.

Another feature to keep in mind is how frustrating the Korean War became. Then as now, Americans wanted quick victories. After General MacArthur's initial advances, Chinese soldiers in large numbers, and flyers from the Soviet Air Force in smaller numbers, helped the North Koreans roll back the United Nations forces to the 38th parallel. For two years and more, here they stayed, producing a situation not unlike the trench warfare of World War I. Reruns of *M*A*S*H* give some idea of how aggravated people felt. It was as if the United States could do nothing but endlessly bang into the same communist-constructed brick wall.

A Man Named Schmuck

Then the pendulum swung in the other direction, but ever so slowly. Before 1953 ended, the sense of an outside threat began to ease. In March, Joseph Stalin died, setting off a power struggle in the Soviet

Union that caused competing communist leaders to back away from an aggressive foreign policy for the next few years. By the summer, President Eisenhower negotiated the truce in Korea he had promised in his presidential campaign, and the fighting ended. On the national scene, in June the execution of the Rosenbergs took place. All of these events helped those on the right wing to calm down.

It took two more years, but then the other side had the satisfaction of witnessing Joe McCarthy's disgrace. Little by little, life looked more promising. It took victories in many small battles to make a difference, and it took years, but it did happen.

My parent's changing fortunes mirrored the nation's. At the very beginning, as mother's job with the Air Force looked more and more in doubt, our house became filled with a sense of disbelief. When she lost it, the anger and frustration came. Once life looked better beyond Bloomfield Street, it started its slow climb upward there as well. For starters, despite all the anger at what had happened and the resolve not to accept it, no internal recriminations took place between Jerry and his sister. I believe he encouraged her and my father to put up a fight and not just walk away from an injustice. Even Nettie held her fire on this issue, maybe because she did not thoroughly understand what had taken place.

I don't know how much information anyone in the house had. If the government officials offered any explanation at all, they told my mother they had fired her under provisions of Public Law 733 passed by the 81st Congress and Executive Order 10450. Based on what they did in other cases, clearly they would have felt no obligation to detail any evidence or explain their actions. The short version is that they considered mother a security risk. That's all they needed in order to fire her.

I assume everyone in the house figured out that Jerry caused the problem. I never heard any discussion about him moving out in order to help mother's effort at reinstatement, but that conversation undoubtedly took place. In fact, at the time, Jerry leaving the house would not have mattered. Given the tenor of the times, I am not entirely convinced his death would have made any difference.

Over time the anger and frustration faded a bit, but the resolve remained. My parents found out that they had the right to appeal the decision, to look for some kind of redress with this internal review. And with Jerry's encouragement, they did.

From what my mother later told me, my father remained particularly determined to see this process through to the end, however far in the future the end might be. In so many ways, that attitude pretty much characterizes my father. He had great difficulty walking away from any undertaking before finishing it. He did everything he could to bring things to their logical conclusion. I think that's why dad so disliked music by the Impressionists Debussy and Ravel. Their music never came to an obvious conclusion; it just stopped.

Given how slowly government machinery churned, Impressionist music seemed like their chosen inspiration. At times mother thought they should just call the whole thing off. Especially after a private sector job did materialize, the emotional stress involved with continuing the appeal process did not seem worth it. As for dad, following his customary way of dealing with the world, he stayed focused on seeing the appeal through to the end, fully believing that vindication would come.

It turns out, he had it right. The Supreme Court provided the key. The old saying is that the members of the court read the election returns. In this mid-century era that is too simplistic a view. After years of basically upholding any law that put national security over personal freedom, by the mid-1950s the Supreme Court under Chief Justice Earl Warren gradually started to roll back its earlier rulings. Around this time "Impeach Earl Warren" signs began appearing along America's highways. Many in Congress desperately wanted the Supreme Court to take back their security rulings and even proposed legislation to make it happen. As Eisenhower's attorney general, William Rogers told him, "the moment [had] long since passed." With the Korean War over, Cold War or no Cold War, the sense of overt danger faded.

In my mother's FBI file sits a memo, dated October 31, 1956, stating the following:

> On 9/24/56 [name crossed out] of the Personnel Security Advisory Committee furnished this Bureau a list of 147 individuals who were seeking restoration to their Government employment as a result of the Supreme Court decision in Cole v. Young on June 11, 1956, in which the Supreme Court held that a Government employee can be dismissed under Executive Order 10450 (Federal Employee Security Program) only if he occupies a sensitive position...

In spite of the male gender used by the author of the memo, mother's name appears on that list of 147 people who appealed, claiming the recent ruling applied to their cases. What about the question of security clearance in mother's case? Since she expressed her willingness to take any civil service position, security clearance no longer mattered.

Despite this promising turn of events, reinstatement proved anything but automatic. It also did not take place with anything remotely resembling deliberate speed. In December 1956 the FBI knew that mother's case was one of thirty-five that needed reinvestigation. Hoover waited until he received a letter (dated April Fools Day, 1957) from the Assistant Chief of the Criminal Investigation Division of the Air Force, requesting FBI help. He then sent a copy to the special agent in charge of the Los Angeles office, accompanied by a one-word message: "Handle." The FBI set out to discover yet one more time whether this presumptuous woman had any direct links to the Communist Party, or alternatively, if she did not, whether any other personal information might prove useful in preventing her re-employment.

In many ways, having tried the first avenue of approach on the initial investigation and failed to find anything, it made sense to put some energy into the second. In the wake of a firing, lapses took place fairly regularly. They included excessive drinking and even criminal behavior of many sorts. Discovering anything along those lines could prevent reinstatement.

In mother's case they could have saved their energy. She never so much as bounced a check, and unlike her mother, she never liked the taste of anything alcoholic. That left the FBI to see if its agents could find what they defined as deviant sexual behavior, by which they meant anything from homosexuality to incest. Evidently, given Jerry's long-term residence in our household, incest looked the most promising. Their final report does not list the questions asked of friends, relations, and neighbors, but it is not all that difficult to fill in the blanks. Take the response given by the mother of one of my school friends who lived down the block, who "stated that she believes that there was a normal [brother/sister] relationship between the employee and [her brother]…"

When all was said and done, the FBI agents did not uncover any other illegal or immoral activities that would prevent reinstatement. Again and again the investigators uncovered what they had found before: No one had any reason to suspect that mother was anything other than an upstanding citizen.

That part of the investigation looks like the FBI's contribution. The Air Force insisted that, despite the Supreme Court ruling, the agents also focus on Jerry's politics and his contact with not just his sister, but other members of our household including me. In April 1957 I had just turned sixteen. No evidence existed that Jerry had been active in left-wing politics beyond 1952 at the very latest. Even if he had, unless mother became actively involved with him, his behavior had no impact on her attempt at reinstatement. I guess the Air Force still wanted to link the two of them in some clear way and paint mother as a communist at heart. The effort proved totally useless.

Perhaps because the pointlessness rapidly became clear, the Bureau did not spend an inordinate amount of time doing the investigation. Before April 1957 ended, they submitted their final report to the Air Force stating, as they usually did in such cases, "This is an FBI investigative report and makes no recommendation for clearance or disapproval."

Out of the thousands of civil service people either fired or forced to resign, mother was one of just a few hundred who got her job back. It took the Air Force until June 30, 1958, to approve mother's reinstatement with pay and benefits, including vacation time, back-dated to December 6, 1954. The man who signed the final documents, the Acting Chief, Administration Branch, L.A. Civilian Personnel Division, had a name I would never have dared to invent: L. A. Schmuck. Yeah, his signature on that document pretty well sums up the description of the government when it came to so-called security cases like my mother's.

From every perspective, her restoration proved no small matter for our family. As mentioned earlier, on a national level, mother became one of only a few hundred people reinstated out of many thousands of victims. Even though my parents did not see the larger picture, on the personal level their victory provided one of the great accomplishments of their lives, and they knew it.

During the whole of my father's adult life, he tried to do something notable his father had not done. Now he had. Yes, dad's employment record, even after mother's restoration, continued to be problematic. I would argue that these problems would have beaten him down if not for the success in mother's case. Her civil service job gave them continual financial security, regardless of my father's employment or lack of it. It took him a few years, but eventually he found a firm of accounts who liked his work. Twenty years on, he retired from that job.

While mother may not have had any real enthusiasm for her work, being able to go back to her government position with a clean record certainly made her feel better about herself. With the award of her back pay and benefits, the consequences of mother's reinstatement went beyond psychological satisfaction. Practically speaking, it meant that if she ever decided to go on the job market, the black mark of disloyalty wouldn't appear on every application she submitted. For two people who never achieved the major ambitions of their lives, they could still take pride in the outcome of their fight for personal vindication. It gave them undeniable evidence of what they could accomplish.

Without their victory, my parents' retirement years would have been quite marginal. Part of that financial triumph for mother involved being able to move to a rather expensive senior citizen community. A long list of relatives joined my parents there. They included Mildred's sister, Pearl and her husband, Nettie's brother, Murray. In addition, Nettie's sister, Bell, and her husband, Henry, also moved in. So did Jerry's second wife, Zelda, and her mother, but only after Jerry died. The family fortress mother always wanted to build became more secure than ever. Getting to that point took almost as much energy as getting mother reinstated.

FIVE

After Shocks

Political and Personal

In some families it might have been possible to keep my mother's and Jerry's problems within the household. Not in ours. Although by the time my immediate family arrived in Hollywood, Jerry said little about his personal situation, mother's close-knit circle of family and friends knew the story. They kept virtually nothing back from one another. Not surprisingly, as the government machinery lurched forward or ground to a halt, mother's dismissal merged with other family discontents. This conflict upset her at least as much as her long, drawn-out efforts at reinstatement. The way she saw it, an extended, unified family provided the best defense against an unpredictable world. If the family fragmented, the world really did become a frightening place.

As mentioned earlier, when it came to politics, the family was far from unified. I guess it is not entirely surprising that both the anti-communists and those who leaned left felt that what happened to mother proved their case. In addition, her fate brought to the surface a whole series of family disputes that had largely remained out of sight until then. They involved people who lived beyond Bloomfield Street and included family members on both coasts. As it turned out, the East Coast branch of my mother's family, especially Lew, spearheaded the movement to get the leftists to repent their misguided views. Those like him, those with a more right-wing outlook, had a limited number of allies on the West Coast, but one proved herself particularly vocal, Uncle Bob's new wife, Sylvia.

While I guess it is not all that unusual for families whose members have known each other for many years to intermarry, it did seem to happen a lot with my family. Sylvia was the sister of Regina, my mother's best friend in high school. A picture of the three of them taken in 1935 shows Sylvia sitting in the middle, smiling broadly, an arm around each of the other two. Mother and Regina are looking uncomfortable and away from the camera. It looks as if Sylvia inserted herself just before the shutter snapped, like they hadn't invited her. Funny how one picture cannot only be worth a thousand words, but can also summarize a lifetime of relationships.

Regina and my mother shared a weight problem, along with the world of low-paid work. Sylvia, the younger sister, led quite a different life. Because of her academic brilliance, Sylvia skipped a couple of grades in grammar school and high school, and then went on scholarship to college. She majored in business, becoming a Certified Public Accountant, a status my father never reached.

Sylvia moved to Los Angeles before we did. She went to work for the United Jewish Appeal (UJA), the parent organization for all the secular Jewish centers located throughout the greater Los Angeles area. By the time my immediate family arrived on the scene, she had become one of the senior officials.

Just because an organization is nonprofit doesn't automatically make its staff or inner workings more humane. UJA didn't necessarily rank kindness to its employees as its primary mission. Like for-profit firms, UJA brought in and distributed many millions of dollars. To raise that money, whenever the opportunity presented itself, the organization twisted arms of small donors as well as large ones. All Jewish center employees, whether full or part time, made a yearly "contribution." No one ever said so in so many words, but everyone involved knew that refusing to contribute wasn't an option. In this atmosphere, Sylvia flourished.

In today's world, when either single or married professional women are the norm, it's easy to forget that, for the 1950s, Sylvia represented something of a rarity. And she knew it; she knew it very well. In order to move up in the working world, Sylvia quickly discovered she needed a hard edge. Kindness equaled weakness. Soft people never rose very high.

To survive and move upward, Sylvia learned to deploy whatever assets she had. The way she looked and presented herself became a major part of that deployment. Her physical appearance tended to intensify the effects of her personality. All her life she remained on the thin side, as if ready for action. Her face had disconcerting features, some of which may have worked to her advantage, some of which did not. Her high cheek bones intensified the visual impact of a large, sensual mouth. On that mouth she wore a badly applied smear of lipstick, as if to say, "I may have to wear what is expected of a woman, but I don't have to like it."

Her eyes also caught people's attention. A wisecrack of the late French president Francois Mitterrand, about the former British Prime Minister, Margaret Thatcher, comes to mind: "The lips of Marilyn Monroe, the eyes of Caligula." Like her British contemporary, rather than use her eyes to introduce a feminine aspect to her image, Sylvia found a way to counter that impression. Those eyes could get exceedingly narrow when she wanted to intimidate someone.

Her voice provided the last weapon. It lay well within the alto range, but with a nasal tone that verged on grating. When she spoke forcefully, it was as if she physically wanted to rub in her opinion. People sometimes agreed with her just to get away from the sound of that voice.

In order to frame this image, Sylvia dressed in expensive, hand-tailored suits complete with shoulder pads rather on the model of the career women portrayed in the movies by actresses like Joan Crawford. That air of formality carried over to recreational events, even when more casual dress would have worked better. Slacks were as casual as she would get.

In the developing battles over politics within the family, Sylvia would not sheave her hard edge. Actually, even in her most personal relationships, that harshness never lay far beneath the surface. At their wedding reception, her new husband, my mother's Uncle Bob, wrapped his arms around her as she passed his chair. He then attempted to pull her on his lap and to give her a kiss. She literally fought her way clear and told him to behave himself.

In many ways, Sylvia had the same kind of logical mind my father did. Perhaps that's why both of them ended up becoming accountants. When it came to talking, however, they showed no similarities. Sylvia, nasal twang and all, spoke out, forcefully.

As for expressing the way she saw the wider world, she very much reflected the views of the Jewish secular establishment of the time. While only the most paranoid American Jews feared a neo-Nazi-inspired American holocaust, a certain general uneasiness remained. At the very least, drifting too far from the U.S. mainstream seemed like an invitation for unwanted attention.

Virtually all of Sylvia's like-minded compatriots supported the creation of Israel, but very few wanted to immigrate there. They were Americans who happened to be born Jewish. Zionist sympathies were the least of their problems in the world. American Jews represented a large portion of the Communist Party. Especially in the 1950s, that was their major problem. Besides, in their view, being a bunch of losers, these communists could conceivably pull other Jews down with them. Sylvia certainly had no intention of becoming one of their victims. She may or may not have known about the internment camps established after 1950 to hold the communists. No matter. Whatever the fate of those headed for disaster, she had no intention of sharing it. The best way to save herself from that fate was to silence them. If that wasn't possible, then Sylvia tried to put as much ideological, and, if necessary, as much physical distance between herself and these dangerous people as she could manage.

Mother's troubles only intensified Sylvia's fears. She knew her recently acquired niece was blameless of any disloyalty to the country. Her innocence only made Sylvia push her anti-communist views more frequently and more loudly than ever. The periodic massed family gatherings gradually became quite tense. Jerry avoided them, and mother became increasingly worried that someone would say something that another family member would find unforgivable. She became especially uneasy when Sylvia and Bob hosted a dinner at their house for the specific purpose of trying to settle the political difference once and for all.

As bright as Sylvia showed herself on various occasions, I don't think she put much thought into creating the right atmosphere to help make her case. Let's start with the meal she served: cold cuts and potato salad straight from the local deli. Unlike the other women in mother's circle, Sylvia took no pride in her cooking. In all fairness, cooking was not one of her strengths, so she couldn't win no matter what she did. Her basic problem was that she had a poor teacher. Belying the stereotype that all Jewish women are good cooks, Sylvia's mother prepared rice for the evening meal by putting it on to boil in the morning.

Regardless of who did the cooking, Sylvia's spread lacked the usual lavishness that the other part-time housewives in the family provided. Sylvia's store-bought meal helped exaggerate the difference between her and the other working women in the family who managed to cook and work. It made her look indifferent to their values and condescending toward them.

Her presentation of the food was not the only barrier Sylvia faced in creating a favorable atmosphere that evening. She and Bob then lived in an expensive, pseudo-Spanish-style apartment building located on the edge of the very Jewish Fairfax district. The family met in her dimly lit living room, decorated with ponderous white furniture and matching white curtains, of a heavy brocaded material, pulled shut over every window. I could just see the other women eyeing the decor and thinking, "No children live in this place." Sylvia's cause was already in some difficulty well before the discussion began.

She did have enough awareness to realize that discussing mother's dismissal and the family members she thought had caused it, would not win her allies. So she decided to focus on the two Jewish leftists who in 1953 found themselves in the most trouble, Julius and Ethyl Rosenberg, the two "atomic" spies who were executed that year. The choice of subject may seem odd, but the innocence of the Rosenbergs had become an article of faith for the Jewish left. For the more liberal members of the family, if the couple's guilt held up, then many other claims made by the anti-communist, anti- Semitic factions would appear much more likely to the wider world. For Sylvia, their guilt motivated her to fight all the more to get the Jews to at least shut up, if not join the anti-communist cause.

At this gathering Sylvia produced all the proof she could muster. She actually brought in pamphlets, articles, and books to support her case. No one had ever done that before at a family gathering. Of equal importance, Sylvia claimed that the Rosenbergs' guilt justified whatever penalty the state imposed on them. Regardless of the evidence then available, her determination to get everyone else to accept the anti-Rosenberg case made the deepest possible impression on the other family members, but not necessarily in the way she wanted to do it.

While on this particular evening she alone came with documentation, it did not over-awe her opponents or cause them to back away from trying to vindicate the Rosenbergs. What her documentation tried to demonstrate ran counter to their instincts on how society should treat Jewish Americans. If the Rosenbergs could be executed, who among them was safe?

In spite of the obvious tensions, everyone behaved civilly, but they did have a debate. Jerry, as usual, did not attend. My mother spoke very little and kept an eye mostly on the tone of the discussion. She would have tried to end it if personal insults started to fly. As I recall, my Republican father, speech defect and all, did say something. He didn't approve of executing the Rosenbergs, whatever he thought of their guilt or innocence. The main burden for the convicted spies' defense fell on Pearl and Murray. I don't think they minded.

As a couple, they intrigued me. They married in 1941, and they moved to L.A. not long afterwards. On the surface, Murray and Pearl did not appear to have much in common, starting with their age. Murray was twenty years older than his wife, and by the time I knew them, a hundred pounds lighter. Like his brothers, Murray had curly black hair, a receding hairline, and the skin pulled very tightly across his thin face. Murray became a printer, the only member of his family to enter that profession. He stuck with the trade all his working life and paid some penalties for his persistence. Long before computerized typesetting became the norm, he endured many years of constantly bending over to select and set type. At first it caused him to become round-shouldered. By the time he reached his sixties, he ended up virtually bent in half. When he took up golf in later years, holding clubs that seemed to tower over him, he presented quite a sight.

He had a personal style unlike anyone else in the family. His early life had been particularly difficult. According to his daughter, as a teenager he had been involved with what was generally called "a rough crowd." At one point he had carried a gun and at least once, someone had taken a shot at him. Perhaps as an echo of his gangster-like past, like the movie villains of the 1930s, Murray wore a snap-brimmed or fedora hat. While I knew him, I thought comedy movies rather than gangster ones acted as his model. He rarely appeared without a cigar in his hand. While talking, in order to punctuate his key point, he would flick the ash with his forefinger at just the right moment. At times he rather reminded me of Groucho Marx, without the eyebrows.

As for his wife, Pearl, she came from a fairly well-to-do Russian Jewish family. They had money to educate their children beyond high school and Pearl became a surgical nurse at Cedars Hospital in Los Angeles. During her L.A. years, she never projected the image of the jolly fat woman; rather, more of a bulldozer. If there was any humor to be found, Murray tended to find it. Pearl came off as much more earnest. Yet whatever their differences in personal style, they found ways to complement each other. Take the way they expressed their left-leaning views. Pearl tended to take the lead, while Murray played the role of her echo, if a somewhat wry one. Their togetherness even extended to recreational activities. As a printer, Murray became conscious of words and how they fit together. Following his lead, they both became very good at Scrabble. In later life they competed in national contests and did rather well.

They died within months of one another, Murray in his nineties, Pearl in her seventies. I never heard them exchange an angry word.

While the words at Sylvia's gathering were not angry, they were plentiful. She and Pearl went at it for a couple of hours. In spite of the lack of voiced anger, I wish I could say that the discussion helped clear the air, but it did not. Neither of these strong-minded women could convince any undecided family members, never mind each other. Did the evening at least produce a grudging respect for one another? Not that I could detect. Instead, if anything, the personal animosity increased and their positions hardened a bit further.

Although I have the impression that Pearl rather enjoyed debate, she had the same instincts that my mother had of putting the family first. If she had to, she could live with personal and political disagreements. Not Sylvia. Periodically over the next twenty years she and Bob would not speak with Pearl and Murray or agree to attend any gathering with those "communists" present. This caused my mother great distress. She kept trying to broker a truce. For short periods of time, she succeeded, but then Sylvia would take off again, with Bob trailing after her.

I could never quite get to the bottom of Sylvia's standoffishness. Most likely part of it came from expecting (and never receiving) deference from the family for her superior accomplishments. But without a stage on which to exhibit her talents, how could she make the others acknowledge her superiority? Perhaps in her mind the danger of associating with vocal left wingers outweighed all other considerations. By the late 1950s it became pretty general knowledge that the FBI watched leftists. A far less intelligent person than Sylvia would have figured out that anyone who consistently associated with such questionable people ran the same risk.

Of course Sylvia's behavior had implications for her husband. Like Lew, Bob was a florist, but there the similarity ends. Bob had a kind of gentleness about him that seemed to fit someone who arranged flowers for a living. He rarely said an unkind word about anyone, even the East Coast wife he divorced before marrying Sylvia. I do recall hearing that during the lengthy family split, secretly Bob would occasionally contact Murray. Pearl wouldn't have cared. If Sylvia found out about it, I have no doubt she knew how to make Bob unhappy for such a betrayal.

Hunting for Security

This split greatly distressed my mother, and she tried desperately to stay on good terms with all members of the family. Having that big, protective, and supportive shield made her feel much less vulnerable and provided a sympathetic audience. In time of troubles, gathering the group tightly about her had special importance. Although she never said so, I suspect she felt guilty that her problems with the government acted as the wedge that began to divide the family.

To my mother, family togetherness was one of the most important aspects of her life. No matter how nasty Sylvia became, mother always tried to keep in contact with her and Bob. Periodically, Sylvia accepted these approaches. At other times, she turned her back and walked away. Given how envious mother was of Sylvia's college education, trying to maintain that contact could not have been easy. Throw in having to deal with the young sister of her best friend now becoming her aunt, and these efforts must have cost mother something. Still, my mother and Bob had always been close. The combination of her desire for family solidarity and affection for him outweighed everything else.

In order to strengthen her shrinking and fractured support system, mother did her best to convince other East Coast family members to move westward. Here she had some good luck and she had some bad. A few of Nettie's and even Barney's relatives did make the move. What mother hadn't anticipated was that, as they arrived, they would get sucked up into the political debates. Rather than helping to smooth over the difference, with the new additions, the political and personal conflict spread.

In 1957, another of Nettie's sisters, Bell, arrived. She was returning to L.A. after having come out with us in 1944. She knew what the place had to offer. Even though she had a nice house near the beach in Far Rockaway, L.A. looked good to her. This time she came with her retired, former ribbon salesman husband, Henry.

Bell was a lively woman, well under five feet tall. In her younger days, she had wanted to become an actress, but her parents would have none of that. Acting was not a proper profession for a young, Jewish woman. Speaking of propriety, early in her life Bell acquired the unfortunate nickname of Pussy. Given the nature of our family and their lack of worldliness about things sexual (at age eighteen, I had to explain to my mother what the terms *satyr* and *nymphomaniac* meant), I can only presume the name did have something to do with Bell's fondness for cats.

Henry was only slightly less vocal than his wife, and they became famous over the years for their verbal duels. These animated discussions often ended with Henry pretending to strangle Bell. As far back as 1934, a close look at the formal, official picture of my parents' wedding dinner reveals Bell and Henry in the far corner taking on just such a pose. Over the years a large number of other snapshots show other family members mimicking them.

Peace and quiet did not have much appeal to either Bell or Henry. Before finally settling into retirement, they bought a liquor store near MacArthur Park in a rough, downtown area of Los Angeles. After various encounters with would-be criminals, they ended up in North Hollywood, living less than a mile away from Pearl and Murray, allied with them in the family struggles.

I'm not sure just what mixture of political principle and personality went into this linkage. Bell and Henry talked a rather conservative line on many social issues, but Bell and Pearl got on well; Bell and Sylvia did not. From my mother's perspective, if Bell was going to choose sides, she had chosen correctly.

At least in California, the women seemed to hold the keys to these relationships. So, a couple of years after Bell and Henry made the journey west, something of a question mark appeared in the form of the last of Nettie's brother's, Sam. Quite unexpectedly he announced that he, too, planned on moving to L.A., and he planned to do it without his wife of many years, Helen. When he arrived on his own, his ultimate destination in the broken family circle remained uncertain for some time. Would he ultimately go back to his wife? Would she follow him out west? Would he remain on his own? Which faction would he choose?

Sam claimed that his personal life had not been happy for some time. He dealt with his discontent by biding his time until after his two adult daughters married. Then he left his wife and came to the West Coast. To inquiring family members he explained that, since the love had gone out of his marriage many years before, he wanted to use his remaining years to create a new life for himself.

Sam never legally divorced his wife, and I don't know what kind of financial arrangement he made for her. Maybe none. I believe she was a reasonably wealthy woman in her own right and kept control of the finances. As a postman, Sam felt this imbalance keenly and it contributed to his sense of frustration. He certainly implied that his wife used her money to dominate their relationship.

As people with egalitarian principles, Pearl and Murray had some natural sympathy for Sam. Besides, in their younger years, the two brothers had gotten along nicely. So Pearl and Murray agreed to let Sam stay with them until he decided what kind of living arrangement he wanted to make. Whether he asked or they offered, I don't know. What I do know is, if he had stayed in Brooklyn, opinion of him would have remained higher.

From the distance of more than forty years, Sam's behavior looks very much like a sad reflection of that rather sad age. Unknown to the hosts, Lew saw a role for Sam to play connected to those housing arrangements.

The idea of communists in the family still troubled Lew. As I mentioned earlier, in his view Jerry had been led astray by Pearl's sister, Mildred. No doubt reinforced by correspondence with Sylvia and Bob, Lew believed that, even though Mildred no longer influenced family affairs, Pearl still did. Although he had not seen either of them for more than a decade, during the 1950s, he confirmed his views with a personal contact. Lew and his wife first visited California not long after we moved into the Bloomfield Street house. They arrived the day a major earthquake thoroughly shook California. They came again in 1956 when, for the first time in years, it rained during the summertime. It seemed like living through a medieval morality play in which nature's displeasure accompanied these visits. Perhaps for Lew, with his theatrical background, it signified he had traveled into the presence of evil.

Even after returning to New York, he wanted to find out just how deeply into the communist system Pearl and Murray had sunk. This is where his brother-in-law, Sam, enters the story. Having Sam act as a household spy seemed like the best way to find out. Yes, it has occurred to me. Their secret little plot is just the kind of behavior that the anti-communists claimed made communist societies so awful.

After less than a year in California, Sam fled to Florida and wrote Lew all the details on what he had uncovered in Pearl and Murray's home, ranging from their reading material to their conversations. I know all this because Lew then wrote a series of letters to family members, including my parents, accusing Pearl and Murray of being agents of the communist conspiracy and the rest of us of aiding and abetting them.

Interestingly, my father set about answering Lew, and a lengthy, political correspondence developed. Unfortunately dad did not save any of these letters, and I can't recall the specific topics they covered. I do remember that in Lew's letters his dramatic instincts often got the better of his evidence. As always, the lack of logic offended my father's sense of fair play. As dad saw it, how could Lew condemn people when he had no evidence their views hurt others? This correspondence with a right-winger who considered himself a socialist also indicates dad's changing politics. In 1960 he voted for Kennedy, not Nixon. Through all that happened in the family, only my father ever changed his political views.

As for Sam, he found a place and a woman in Miami Beach. He died there in 1968. His estranged wife brought his body back to New York City where I attended his funeral service. The rabbi, who did not know the family at all, spoke from a prepared text that I presume he used at other such events. Unfortunately, he emphasized what a good and loyal husband Sam had been, while not failing to touch upon the devotion he showed to his daughters and grandchildren. In fact, Sam had not seen any of them in years. When these comments sent up great wails and a flood of tears from Sam's wife and daughters, the rabbi figured he had hit his target and just laid it on even thicker.

This sorry tale is further evidence for my firmly held belief that only two "philosophers" ever figured out how the modern world works. One is Woody Allen and the other is Mel Brooks. This New York funeral is pure Woody Allen.

It would have pleased my mother greatly if Sam's death had acted as the ending point to all the family discontent. That was one wish she did not get. For the rest of her life, Sylvia continued to reappear and then vanish in a huff for reasons that were difficult to anticipate. Often as not, they had nothing to do with politics. Especially in front of my mother, Peal and Murray remained polite to Sylvia and Bob, but bitingly sarcastic about their adversaries when mother left. Lew remained convinced that he had done his duty by calling attention to the communist menace within the family. The best mother could do was keep the lines of communication open to both camps. Despite her best efforts, they never reconciled.

Through the fights and the reconciliations and the renewed combat, Jerry managed to remain aloof. Even for the smaller dinner parties, he chose his company carefully. He decided he needed to keep his political ideas to himself, even in sympathetic company. I don't know if he had come to the conclusion that his cause was hopeless, or if by staying quiet, he hoped the system would not inflict any further punishment on him. As it turned out, he couldn't control his own destiny. While my mother's troubles grew and festered, while the family divided and fought, the forces on the right decided to make one more effort to make Jerry pay for his communist past.

Barny & Nettie 1906

Nettie with brothers and sisters 1904

George with my father and a sister 1910

My father 1934

My mother 1934

My mother, Sylvia and Regina 1930s

Jerry and Mildred 1944

Nettie Toasting

Gene Kelly in Pal Joey 1941   *Charlie Chaplin and Oona Chaplin 1946*

Jerome Robinson Theatrical Phtographs collection, Department of Special Collections, Chearles E. Young Reasearch Library, UCLA

Pearl and Murray 1942

Sam at the beach 1940s

Lew carving 1940s

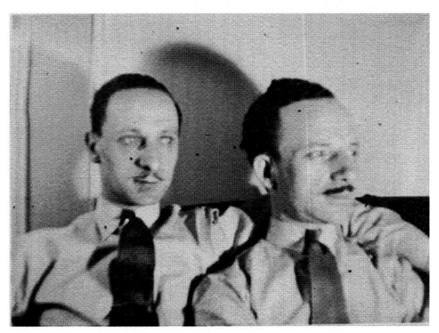

Bob and Murray 1930s

SIX

A Pinch of Incense

The Many Sides of Paranoia

In the spring of 1953, Jerry came into the house and said that he had left his wallet on the seat of his fire-engine-red convertible, and someone apparently had taken it. Not much money was involved, but he did have to go through the inconvenience of getting a copy of his driver's license and of canceling a gasoline company credit card. None of these matters particularly concerned him. Another one did, however: "the telegram" from Congressman Harold Velde he kept in his billfold for "safe keeping" had vanished along with everything else. Velde had recently taken over as chair of the House Un-American Activities Committee and had subpoenaed Jerry to appear at the hearings the committee planned to hold in Los Angeles. The telegram gave him the updated information on when and where he should appear.

Through withdrawal and silence Jerry may have wanted to put his active political life behind him. Congressman Velde had other ideas. Forcing Jerry out of his job at the movie studios did not end the anti-communist faction's interest in him. The obvious question is, why?

With all the results from using the Freedom of Information Act spread out before me, this renewed interest in Jerry looks suspicious. It comes at about the same time the first FBI investigation of my mother took place. Although friends and neighbors mentioned to her that FBI agents had been around asking questions, at the time no one in our house made the connection with the House Un-American Activities Committee subpoena. As far as the family was concerned, Jerry's former political activism had no relationship to the security check on mother. Looking back on all of this, quite naturally, the first thought to pop into my mind is that a connection, a scheme, existed. Calling Jerry to testify just had to play a part in the effort to have mother fired as a security risk. Well, let's see.

Where would such a plot have begun? Not with the committee. Even leaving to one side its dependence on the FBI for a lot of its information, it had other problems as well. Organization was the first one. After winning control of the House of Representatives in the November 1952 elections, the new Republican majority needed to throw out the Democratic committee chairs and appoint their own. That's why it wasn't until early 1953 that Velde, the committee's new Republican chair, had any opportunity to shape the agenda to his liking. People as ordinary as Jerry and my mother were hardly likely to be his first priority. No, if a plot existed, it began with the FBI.

Mother's FBI file contains one major report from early 1953. This is the one that deals with Jerry's activities in detail, as well as those of my mother through all of her working life. It's dated February 26, 1953. A week and a half later, on March 9, her file has a supplementary report correcting that false information about signing the petition sponsored by the Communist Party in Cleveland. The agent submitting the report to Hoover mentions that he checked the files of the House Un-American Activities Committee to see if mother's name appeared there. The agent reports that it did not.

If it ever occurred to the agent to check on Jerry as well, that information did not make it into the version report I saw. It's hard to believe that if the agency planned to use a committee appearance by Jerry to help discredit mother, some comment on the plan would not have shown up here. Yet funny things happen to individual files, so I checked further.

Looking at the possible plotting from another direction, I checked out Jerry's file for early 1953. A note to Hoover dated March 20 from what looks like the same agent in the Los Angeles office who reported on mother, announced that the day before the committee had subpoenaed Jerry. Actually, this was the second subpoena. For reasons I'll discuss later, committee members now wanted him to appear in April, not March. What is more important, in this brief note mother is not mentioned.

While it is true that portions of this document are blacked out in my copy, attempts at censorship proved rather inconsistent. When it came to documents sent through Freedom of Information requests, different FBI offices had different redaction practices. That is how I know these portions involve the name of the Special Agent in Charge of the Los Angeles Office (Carlson) and the name of the committee source that gave the information to the FBI (Wheeler). Still, in all the documents I saw in Jerry's file from these few months, mother's name did not appear.

Like it or not, based on the available information, it doesn't look as though Jerry's appearance before the House Un-American Activities Committee had anything to do with the investigation of my mother. Yet even if no advance plotting took place, they could still possibly, belatedly, have made the linkage. They could have then discredited mother by using the committee's subpoena of Jerry as evidence of current subversive behavior.

Here she had a bit of good luck. Even though Carlson and Hoover exchanged information, they never made the connection between Jerry testifying before the committee and mother's case. I would have been surprised and impressed if one of them had recognized the coincidental link. They both dealt with a large volume of cases every day, and since my mother's case would hardly rank as a major investigation, why would either of them have noticed?

From the look of things, timing may have had something to do with the missed connection as well. The key question is, when did the list of people (including Jerry) scheduled to testify before the committee reach the FBI? That trail began not long before March 6. On March 6, the people in the L.A. office of the FBI found the committee investigator, William Wheeler, at their door requesting:

> cooperation to extent of furnishing addresses, if known of twenty[-]nine individuals for whom HCUA is contemplating issuing subpoenas for forthcoming hearings. Majority of these are or have been connected with radio, cartoonists, music or acting industry in Hollywood. Basis for Wheeler's compilation of these names unknown but Wheeler admits he does not have specific evidence against them...

Despite a sarcastic remark by Hoover in the margin about Wheeler's request that the L.A. office could help out only if it had the time, its agents came through quickly because Jerry's first subpoena went out on March 7.

In a report filed a week later, Jerry's name is mentioned specifically as one of this group. He is listed as a photographer, alphabetically right after David and Naomi Robison, also residents of

North Hollywood. By this time the FBI agents in the L.A. office were no longer conducting an active investigation of my mother and had moved on to other matters. The final report on her case from Washington is dated March 17.

Someone once said that, while it may be more satisfying to find orderly plots behind unpleasant events, in nine cases out of ten, look at coincidence or incompetence to find the real explanations. In Jerry and my mother's case that anonymous someone gave good advice. Taking everything into account, coincidence does explain what happened quite nicely, and from the FBI's perspective, bad luck explains missing the linkage. Incompetence is not a fair charge for failing to make the connection.

Does this missed opportunity matter? Since the FBI investigation convinced the Air Force to suspend mother anyway, the link with the Un-American Activities Committee made no difference in the outcome. Yet, for the committee and for the FBI, it could have mattered. The main interest of both groups was publicizing their successes in rooting out subversives. An appearance before that committee often resulted in a matchless level of notoriety. That association would have put a vivid exclamation point on mother's investigation and given opportunities for issuing more press releases about successful thwarting of the communist menace.

J. Edgar Hoover's Lament

So going back to the original question, if having my mother fired from her Air Force job didn't motivate the House Un-American Activities Committee to call Jerry, what did? The best way to find the answer to that question is to widen the search and look at how the anti-communist forces on the committee, with Hoover's FBI hovering nearby, operated in the early 1950s.

The first point to make is that no one had a grudge against Jerry. Personal vendettas played no part in creating the committee's witness list. Given the harsh treatment some witnesses received, and what their appearance before the committee did to their lives, that may sound implausible. Yet it is true. To the authorities, it was nothing personal. That was the problem. They did not care even a little bit about the personal impact on their witnesses/victims. Once again, Jerry found himself caught up in a nationwide, anti-communist hysteria, just like his sister.

In looking at how the committee treated these people and why it acted the way it did, I realize that it is as easy for me to fall into a trap. It's the trap of seeing all those on the political right as operating in lock-step, rather like those people who shook their fists at me in that Indiana political gathering. Yet it is impossible to read the correspondence or hear transcripts and not acknowledge that those on the right had differences of principle and of personality. When looking at the House Un-American Activities Committee, that point showed up again and again.

In 1951, the committee reopened its operations in Hollywood and once more began investigating those in the film industry. Hoover did cooperate with the committee—selectively cooperate would be a better way to put it. He still wanted to use the hearings as a device for punishing the opposition; so did the committee.

But the FBI director had a much different standard of punishment than did committee members. As a result, his dealings with the committee and its members ran anything but smoothly. His attitude had not changed since the days of the Deis Committee. He wanted the lion's share of the credit for whatever took place on the anti-communist front, and he wanted the committee focused on the people and places that he thought were important.

In pursuit of that goal, the imprisoned congressman Thomas was far from the only committee person with whom the FBI director clashed. Hoover ran into a whole series of committee people and incidents that frustrated and angered him, starting with Richard Nixon.

In September 1948, the press quoted the young congressman as saying that the committee accomplished more in rooting out government subversives in three days of hearings than the FBI had accomplished in eight years. While Nixon subsequently apologized to one of Hoover's associates for the remark—a misquote, or so he said—the letter detailing the conversation has two handwritten comments on it. One states that Nixon's strategy is designed to bring him headlines, and the other claims: "Nixon plays both sides against the middle." To which Hoover added a two-word note: "I agree."

Relations with committee staff proved equally touchy and also prompted handwritten, marginal commentary by the FBI director. In 1950 the investigator, Wheeler, wanted information about a suspected Honolulu communist involved in a court case that the FBI had done a great deal to bring to trial. Here the note reads: "This is outrageous. We should promptly advise Dept. [of Justice] as case is on appeal." The FBI also had problems with the committee counsel, Frank Tavenner. When he first signed on as a staff member in 1949, the Richmond, Virginia, FBI office gave him an enthusiastic endorsement as "friendly...toward the Bureau and its personnel." Four years later, after a continuing series of disagreements about viewing FBI files, a memo now said that nothing would be accomplished while Tavenner held his current post. The same memo proposed demoting him. Once again, Hoover noted, "I certainly agree."

At first glance, with the Republican presidential and congressional victories in the November 1952 elections and Velde taking over as committee chair, it might look like relations would improve. After all, the new chair had once been an FBI agent. In fact, Hoover and Velde were bound to clash. Now, as a congressman and chair of an important committee, Velde looked forward to a degree of independence and to making a name for himself that he lacked as an anonymous FBI agent. He had a surprise coming.

Hoover balked at letting his former employee and committee staff personally make use of FBI files, even if Velde demoted Tavenner. As Hoover put it, "...there had not been as close a coordination with the House Un-American Activities Committee as I believed there should have been." Just in case the new chair wondered, J. Edgar Hoover demonstrated quite forcefully to him that his once and future boss remained the same person.

The Question

Even with all of these background struggles of allies within the anti-communist movement, none of which were known to the public at the time, the committee developed a trademarked style of dealing with its witnesses. This style had the effect of disrupting the activities of many groups and established organizations of the political left, and it did so quite effectively. If it had not been so effective, the complaints about the committee would not have grown so loud.

What happened in Hollywood provides a case study of this style of operation that worked equally well for the disruption of unions, churches, and civil rights groups. From 1951 onward, Hollywood communists and former communists appeared before the committee or one of its subcommittees. Although big names continued to make occasional appearances, the committee abandoned its initial policy of all stars, all the time. Now they wanted to show how deeply the communist menace had penetrated the entertainment industry in Hollywood. That is why Jerry ended up with a subpoena in his wallet.

The witnesses the committee members brought before them, even non-famous ones, faced ever-increasing levels of publicity. What's more, the coverage came from a wide variety of media. In that pre-cable television, pre-Internet age, most movie theaters used Movietone News to present about five to ten minutes of headline news to the audience before the movie began. This way the faces of well-known witnesses, as well as lesser figures, reached millions. So did the faces and voices of committee members. In addition, the number of television sets continued to grow rapidly, replacing radio and the movies as a source of information and entertainment. And committee members were well aware of this increased exposure. As a result, the local television stations often carried live broadcasts of at least part of the committee hearings, and the national television news programs had bits and pieces as well. Last, but not least, sympathetic newspapers, like the *Los Angeles Times* and those in the Hearst chain, carried daily pictures and stories about the hearings.

Before media of every description, inevitably, committee witnesses had to face the question, the one forever linked to the House Un-American Activities Committee: "Are you now or have ever been a member of the Communist Party?" Just weeks before World War II ended, John Howard Lawson toyed with the idea of simply admitting to the committee that he was a communist and in effect daring the members to do something about it. By 1951, admitting to current membership proved rare. As mentioned earlier, under the terms of the 1940 Smith Act, even mere membership in the Communist Party could be considered criminal behavior. For the select group of witnesses who appeared before the committee, prosecution seemed like a real possibility.

Even admitting past membership presented problems for witnesses. If they answered that they had formerly been members, no matter how briefly, no matter how long ago, then the committee members and staff had the legal right to ask them the names of other people who belonged to the party. The witnesses could not refuse to name others without risking a criminal contempt citation from the committee. This power to jail or to fine witnesses also left them with little or no legal means to overturn a contempt citation. At this time the Supreme Court ruled that once individuals had waived their Fifth Amendment right to self incrimination, they could not try to protect other people who may have been involved in criminal behavior.

In some ways, what the committee did to its witnesses rather reminds me of a scene from the first act of George Bernard Shaw's play *Androcles and the Lion*. Here the pagan Roman captain tells the beautiful, condemned Christian, Lavinia, that all she has to do is drop a pinch of incense onto the fire in a Roman temple in either a public or private ceremony. For that small price, her condemnation would vanish, and her life would return to normal.

What's In a Name?

More than one author writing on the subject of the House Un-American Activities Committee has pointed out that naming names had the same kind of ritualistic function as Shaw's pinch of incense. I don't disagree. When dealing with those on the political right, ritual is often a key element in their worldview. That said, what happened at committee hearings went beyond ritual. Appearance before the committee proved much more devastating to the individuals than just forcing them to participate in an unwanted ceremony. As everyone knew, naming someone put that person's job at risk, especially if that individual had not previously revealed membership in the Communist Party. By demanding that witnesses name others with similar views to their own, the committee sowed division and hard feelings. These people had privately cooperated with one another to achieve what they thought were worthwhile ends. If their names became public, they felt betrayed by their former friends and allies.

Acquaintances, neighbors, and relations could and did give those identified as communists a hard time. Just look at my family. Some witnesses tried to avoid these consequences for themselves and their friends by naming dead people or people whom others had mentioned. Not unexpectedly, the dead people's close relations and friends did not appreciate the public exposure. Dead people could no longer offer an explanation for past behavior. As for the living already named, that person often felt a renewed sense of betrayal each time their name received public mention once again at a committee hearing.

Why not just stand behind the Fifth Amendment and say, "I refuse to answer that question on the grounds that it might incriminate me?" Because, to a certain extent, "Fifth Amendment Communists" helped the committee just as much as those who named names. They demonstrated that the Red Menace remained alive and well. In much of the public's view, those using the Fifth Amendment confessed their communist sympathies. If they didn't have them, why not just deny membership in front of the committee? The other vital consideration in using the Fifth Amendment concerned the witness's own job and its likely loss. If the committee identified a person as a current or former member of the Communist Party or if membership was implied by pleading the Fifth, the studio would fire that individual. The movie company executives claimed they did not fire former members. Although no one believed them, they told a partial truth. If an individual agreed to admit membership, express regret, and name others, then the film industry bosses agreed to keep sending projects to their retreaded patriot. Hence, there was reluctance to plead the Fifth and an incentive to name names.

When it comes to naming names, many examples come to mind, but a couple are worth mentioning here. The first is well known: the director Elia Kazan. He named more than a few. As a result, Kazan alienated other Hollywood figures so deeply that, forty years later when he received a special Academy Award for his accomplishments in film, a large number of those present at the ceremony refused to rise or applaud when the presenter announced his name. (Even the supportive and rather intimidating appearance of Robert De Niro standing next to Kazan wasn't enough to get them to rise.)

The other example is much less well known: Meta Reis Rosenberg, Jerry's neighbor from Beachwood Drive. After her appearance before the committee, she left the movies for a highly successful career in the greener (meaning both newer and more profitable) pastures of television, where she often teamed up with Roy Huggins. Perhaps coincidentally, perhaps not, he had a similar history left-wing views to hers when he took the stand in committee hearings and named people.

The rise of television provides an important part of the background to the way the studios and many others connected with the movie industry reacted to the committee's probe of Hollywood communist activity. The Supreme Court ruled that the studios could not own local movie theaters. That ruling broke up the movie moguls' monopoly, so the challenge of television caught them at a weak time. They needed to keep the services of, and protect the reputations of, their proven money-makers, including stars, directors, and even writers. Naming communists before the committee meant these walking dollar signs then became members in good standing of the patriotic community. The American Legion would not sponsor boycotts of their films or picket them at the local movie theaters. Of equal importance, the New York bankers, who financed films, would advance the needed funds so the movie industry could produce them. No wonder the Hollywood establishment put pressure on their box office champions to get "clearance" by appearing before the committee and naming those names.

Others besides the studio executives actively applied this pressure as well, including the actors' agents who represented these money-makers. Pretty obviously 10 percent of nothing is nothing. So more than one agent refused to willingly let lucrative clients sabotage their own careers because of something as nebulous as principle.

No one will be surprised to learn that lawyers greased the wheels of this process, especially one named Martin Gang. He had developed relationships with committee staff members such as Frank Tavenner and William Wheeler, and he used them. These connections are not as strange as they might seem. Wheeler had served as one of the Secret Service agents who guarded President Franklin Roosevelt. More important, he described himself as a Democrat who later wondered if his role with the committee was a good idea. As for Tavenner, Hoover knew his enemies.

To complete this group and cover all possible angles, a former communist and current mental health therapist named Phil Cohen entered the picture. Since the true nature of his role did not surface for several years, he could help convince his clients to testify as a so-called friendly witness. His client could name those names, all in the interest of mental health.

Meta Reis Rosenberg is a poster child for all these connections. Her husband, George, was an agent. He was friendly with Gang, Cohen, and Wheeler. Along with a couple of Hearst newspaper reporters, they went to football games together when the Rams played football in L.A.

Hoover evidently took a dim view of this idea that confession led to redemption. In 1951, when a memo reached him filled with optimism about the lengthy and informative testimony of Rosenberg and others before the committee, the FBI director's sour, handwritten notation read, "So far the so-called 'full disclosures' appear to have been self serving & solely for [the] purpose of getting a committee 'whitewash.'"

Hoover could see no way to go from purgatory to heaven. For him purgatory didn't exist. Reds should go to hell. At this stage, he proved unwilling to acknowledge that creating a culture in which those on the left who turned on one another, or at the very least agonized about it, did as much damage to his enemies as anything the FBI did to them. As it turns out, Nixon probably had it right. Three days of left wingers testifying before the committee did their cause more damage than anything the FBI had done to them.

The political as personal

From this distance, looking at all the activity at once, it is easy to overlook each targeted person's agony. A portion of a letter from Howard Koch to a friend of his living in England shortly after this period should help to bring it back:

> I should point out…that as a last resort appearing before a member of the Committee is no longer an impossible procedure to contemplate. It depends, I should say, on how skillfully one is able to walk the tight-rope, balancing between what they want and what you're willing to say. It's not a question of being asked to name names—that's out with us…the Committee has all the names. I happen to feel there are other ways of disavowing ideas and friends besides calling them Communists. I realize there can be honest differences of opinion on this question but I can't but feel that in renouncing past beliefs there is a danger of finding oneself with a whole new set of premises that require more of a psychological adjustment than one is aware of in the beginning.…

The reasons for his anguish are clear. Before this letter went out, Koch had received the full treatment. The studios and even television networks refused his scripts. Studio executives told him he needed to clear himself before the committee, and they even forced him to talk with Martin Gang. Koch never did appear before the committee. For the next five years, he and his wife settled in England.

Yet what of those who stayed, appeared before the committee, and refused to turn on their friends and risked getting jailed for contempt of congress? What of those who decided to use the Fifth Amendment as their defense? These people came in various shapes and sizes. Some had no problems admitting that at some stage of their life, for a few years, they joined the Communist Party. They also admitted they became disillusioned with what they found there, and then quit. The committee considered such statements as half a loaf. Unless the witness willingly named others, the stamp of "unfriendly" went out with the press release describing that witness's behavior.

The playwright Lillian Hellman became one of the best-known people to have this attitude and to use that strategy. She proposed to the committee that she would testify that she was not currently a member of the Communist Party. Then, gradually, in response to questioning, she would "retreat" year by year until she got to the last year in which she last held a membership. At this point she planned to use the Fifth Amendment. The committee refused to play the game by her rules. But much to the fury of its members, Hellman got the advantage of them anyway by widely distributing a letter at the hearing just before she testified. This letter laid out her political views and why she held them.

Some witnesses did attempt to toy with the committee. Presumably they felt they could avoid a contempt citation or did not care if they did some jail time. The actor Lionel Stander said he could name "a group of fanatics who are desperately trying to undermine the Constitution" and then named the members of the House Un-American Activities Committee he then faced. The North Hollywood housewife Naomi Robison actually flustered one of the congressmen so thoroughly by her responses that he felt the need to blurt out that he was not against motherhood.

Brief Encounter

Keeping all of this background in mind, Jerry's appearance before the committee presents some puzzles. The first is Congressman Velde. As late as March 9, he wrote the people at Movietone News, who wanted to have live footage of the hearings in Los Angeles, which he planned to attend.

In fact a subcommittee of Republican Donald Jackson and Democrat Clyde Doyle heard Jerry's testimony along with Tavenner, Wheeler, and a clerk to take the notes. The two congressmen represented L.A. districts and both sported reputations as noted conservatives. Tavenner knew a demotion awaited him, so his feelings about his participation and his attitude toward witnesses remain something of a question.

In this case as in so many others, the ever-busy Wheeler dug up virtually all of the information the committee used. According to documents provided by the National Archives from the committee's files, Jerry originally should have appeared at a public hearing on the morning of March 23 at the Federal Building in Los Angeles. Instead he showed up for a private executive session with only subcommittee members and staff present in the Cleveland Room of the Statler Hotel at 9:15 in the evening.

The full record of the hearing goes like this: after asking if Jerry had a lawyer with him (he did not) and asking about his educational and work background Tavenner asked:

> The committee has information, Mr. Robinson, that in 1944 you were a member of a branch of the Communist Party in Los Angeles? Is that correct?

Mr. Robinson.	I decline to answer that question.
Mr. Tavenner.	On what grounds do you decline?
Mr. Robinson.	The Fifth Amendment, I guess.
Mr. Tavenner.	I see no occasion for my asking any additional questions.
Mr. Jackson.	Any questions, Mr. Doyle?
Mr. Doyle.	No questions.
Mr. Jackson.	Is there any reason why the witness shouldn't be excused?
Mr. Tavenner.	No.
Mr. Jackson.	You are excused.
Mr. Robinson.	Will you need me again?
Mr. Jackson.	No. You are excused from your subpena.[sic]...

Calling what took place in that hearing room perfunctory is something of an overstatement, but it will do. The committee could have pressed Jerry about other members of the communist groups to which he belonged in New York and Los Angeles. They could have tried to find out about his role in the Joint Anti-Fascist Refugee Committee and who had helped him. None of that happened. The committee's dependence on Wheeler had a lot to do with that absurdly brief hearing.

Earlier I mentioned that Jerry's name appeared on the committee's witness list rather belatedly and in combination with nearly thirty other people. At the time, Wheeler did not even know the addresses of all the people he wanted to appear as witnesses, including Jerry. It was his custom, whenever possible, to question potential witnesses before they appeared at a committee hearing. An unpleasant surprise from a witness was the last thing members wanted in front of live television coverage. In this case, I don't think Wheeler had the time to provide them with that protection. He asked for the information from the FBI on March 6, and according to the notation in the committee file at the National Archive, the subpoena went out the next day. In that same file, under Jerry's name, this is all that is recorded: "Investigation of communist infiltration in Hollywood has developed that you were a member of Branch A of the Communist Party in the year 1944. Is that correct?" It sounds like Wheeler had little time to do much more than find out Jerry's name. Most likely a woman named Judith Raymond provided it. She had attended a party gathering hosted by Jerry and Mildred. In September 1953, like Jerry, she appeared in an executive session before the committee.

At Jerry's hearing the subcommittee did not ask him about all of his activities in the party before he came to Los Angeles, nor did its members question him about the Joint Anti-Fascist Refugee Committee, because they did not have that information. The FBI had only given them Jerry's Bloomfield Street address. Leaving to one side the time problem, Hoover was still in the process of teaching Congressman Velde his manners.

The committee did have three "official" reasons for holding an executive session. They claimed that they used this technique when the testimony about people other than the witness would prove defamatory, or when classified information might be revealed, or, more vaguely, when public testimony might negatively impact "the national interest." None of these reasons fit Jerry's case. The committee's lack of staff does.

Judging by a letter Velde wrote about this time to Senator Karl Mundt of South Dakota, a former member of the committee, Velde had a thin skin and particular sensitivity to attacks in the press. Putting witnesses before the television cameras and newspaper reporters live, without knowing their testimony in advance, looked risky to the congressman.

It just made more sense to hear Jerry in executive session. From the committee's point of view, with luck, that hearing could produce a positive outcome. If the appearance frightened Jerry enough, with little prompting, he might name others. Then they could schedule an open hearing with him as a cooperative witness. The delay needed to set up a second hearing would give Wheeler more time to gather additional information. As it turned out, thanks to Jerry's one-line negative reply, the committee didn't manage to accomplish anything of the sort.

Jerry's concern about the lost telegram shows he took what was happening to him seriously. Afterwards he did not say much about what went on in the hearing room or how he felt about the way they treated him. All he ever said to me about his appearance before the committee was that these people wanted him to give them his friends' names and he wouldn't do it. As the record of the hearing shows, they never advanced that far in their questioning to ask him about others, but his judgment about why they wanted him there is no doubt on target. The committee had name collection in mind for virtually all its witnesses.

I think Jerry knew very well how lucky he had been in his dealings with them, and how easily he got off. At the time he could not have known all the reasons for his relative good fortune. Unlike so many other witnesses, the committee had little or no financial leverage. The studio had already fired him. Granted, cooperation might have resulted in his reinstatement. As one whose income even in the best of times at the studios fell far short of Gene Kelly's or Howard Koch's, reinstatement would have made little practical difference to the way he lived. Sometimes being a little fish swimming with sharks means that the little fish is not considered a full meal, and survives.

So exactly what did Jerry do in 1953 to survive in the real world? He still worked as a photographer, but he had his schemes and dreams.

Seven

Making It

Return to Broadway

The theater always attracted Jerry more than the movies. While I knew him, he seldom went to the movies. Even leaving professional assignments aside, he surrounded himself with theater, especially musical theater. When we arrived in L.A. in 1950, all his albums spun at the then innovative speed of 33⅓ rpms. But what really impressed me was that they took up multiple shelves of a bookcase. He had many of the musicals he had photographed on Broadway: *Pal Joey*, *On Your Toes*, *Roberta*, and each year it kept growing.

While I would not say he spent hours and hours with me discussing these musicals, still as I grew in my teenage years, we sometimes listened together. When I wanted his opinion about a show, he could give it with no small amount of knowledge behind what he said. He would make comments about the dialog and how it fit with the structure of the music and about the lyrics, and why he thought the combination did or did not work. He had a strong awareness of how the music, lyrics, and story blended together because, aside from the records, he also bought many of the scripts just as soon as Samuel French published them.

Jerry's interest in the musical theater led him beyond collecting records and scripts. His initial Communist Party grouping in Hollywood with the writers' group is an early indicator. When he first arrived on the West Coast, I don't think a lack of alternatives caused party officials to pick that group for him. The FBI believed Jerry earned some of his living from writing as well as photography, but the agents' reports never went into detail about what he wrote. It turns out, for some time, he had wanted to write a musical.

By 1950, he had written a musical comedy called *Nefretiti*. For years he kept a plaster copy of that strikingly beautiful ancient Egyptian queen's head on display in our living room. I don't know where he first ran across his subject. Maybe her beauty first attracted Jerry's attention. Whatever the source of his interest, he had done his research and knew that in real life the queen and her husband did some things that were not so pretty. He also knew that despite these limitations, the queen had come very much into fashion at that time, and he hoped to latch onto her fame.

When it came to the finer points of putting a play together, I'm not sure whether or not Jerry ever had any training, formal or otherwise. Given his interests and what he did for a living, he had something of a head start in learning the basics. He wouldn't have been the first successful playwright to get his start that way. However, I do have one speculation about another possibility; he may have done some studying with a man named Abe Burrows.

Among other works, Burrows co-authored the musical *Guys and Dolls*, but even before that hit, he had the reputation as a script doctor, a man who fixed up bad scripts. In 1943 Burrows ended up in Hollywood fixing up movie scripts. He also taught radio comedy writing for an outfit known as the People's Education Center, a front group of the Hollywood Communist Party. Specifically, they hired him to teach shipyard workers. Jerry, of course, worked in the shipyards at that time. Granted, a Broadway play is not a radio program, but Jerry saw *Nefretiti* as a comedy, and he most assuredly belonged to the Communist Party.

To be a hit, his play needed both memorable music and memorable comedy. I never heard the score, but I think Jerry had some doubts about the comedy. I can remember him speaking about one of the gags involving an ancient Egyptian messenger coming to the queen and announcing, "Hail, I bring greetings from the President of the United States!" He felt a bit defensive about that line and tried, unconvincingly, to justify using it. Taking the play as a whole, I think he had reasons for his uneasiness. The balance seemed off.

Perhaps his lack of confidence in the humor led him to use only a minimum of dialog. Instead of talk, using a variety of shows such as *On Your Toes, Oklahoma,* and *Carousel* as his models, he relied on the ballet to tell a good part of the story. While for *On Your Toes,* that device worked pretty well, I thought it was overdone in *Nefretiti*.

Such a weakness did not make the play hopeless—far from it. Other shows have started out with bigger handicaps, and perhaps this one was not beyond repair. What Jerry needed was an Abe Burrows–like script doctor to take it on as a project. Then as now, it was not easy to find that kind of help for someone doing a first play, especially someone who had yet to find financial backing.

In an effort to beat those odds, Jerry did something he had never done before. In the summer of 1956 he hosted a pool party for a large number of his theater and motion picture friends. Among the people he asked was the recently returned Howard Koch.

Of all the exiled, blacklisted, writers Koch and his wife probably did about as well as any of them. She wrote under an assumed name for a Robin Hood television series produced in England and sold to the U.S. market. He did movie writing over there under the pseudonym of Peter Howard. They both associated with others on the black list, such as the director Joseph Losey, and Charlie Chaplin and his wife.

In June 1956, thanks to a Supreme Court ruling, the U.S. State Department rather reluctantly and unexpectedly renewed Koch's passport after first trying to confiscate it. He took the opportunity to return to the United States. Once back, a lawyer named Edward Bennet Williams fixed it so Koch cleared himself from the black list without having to go before the House Un-American Activities Committee.

It took a while for Williams to work his magic. After he did, Koch could write for Hollywood again using his own name, and, equally important to him, receive the money he deserved. During this interlude and for some years after, Koch had no intention of living in the movie capital. Instead, after a brief visit to L.A., he moved to Woodstock, New York, well before it became a world-famous concert location. There he planned to concentrate on Broadway, at least until his clearance came through. Of interest to Jerry, Koch wanted to produce as well as write plays. Whether or not Jerry sent him his play before the party took place, I do not know. I do recall Koch wandering about the edge of the pool, but seldom speaking to anyone. In the end, Jerry's project failed to interest him, and from that time on, I never heard anything more about trying to get it produced.

Seeing Them Dance in the Dark

While these efforts to become a successful playwright periodically occupied Jerry, he still had to make a living. He did so once again from plays other people wrote. After losing his job with the movie studios, he put full-time effort into photography at the Pasadena Playhouse. For the general public beyond the L.A. area, this grouping of theaters is little known, but for those all over the country in the profession of drama, its name will produce at least a nod of recognition. The playhouse was and is unique, and what Jerry did there was unique as well.

Two men, Gilmor Brown and Charles Prickett, created the Pasadena Playhouse. They began with a set of community players in Pasadena. By 1924 the two of them had successfully gathered the funds to create a theater school that stood on its own and had no connection to a college or university. Over the years the physical structure grew to the point where it had a main stage and associated little theaters like the Playbox.

Notice I described it as a theater school. Besides doing main stage production with "names" in the leading roles, it also trained young actors and actresses along with the full supporting staff that every production needed. Since the playhouse stood so close to Hollywood, Brown and Prickett saw to it that they prepared their students for the movies as well. Eventually they added a television production team to the mix. Given how long it has operated, the list of its graduates would take up many pages, but a few connected with Jerry are worth pointing out.

One was a slightly built blond fellow named John Mantley. If his name as an actor does not ring any bells, his work as a producer might. The long-running television program *Gun Smoke*, starring fellow Pasadena Playhouse graduate James Arness, is his best-known production. I met Mantley at Jerry's Hollywood Boulevard house one afternoon in the late summer of 1950. He had come to pick up some pictures, but when he arrived, he found Jerry in the darkroom still working on the prints. Although Mantley seemed like a rather shy man, he struck up a conversation with me while he waited. At that time he had the title role in a commercial production of *Cyrano de Bergerac;* presumably, that was why he entered the house with two fencing foils under his arm. He very kindly gave me, at age nine, my one and only fencing lesson. Jerry did finally emerge, prints in hand, to save this patient actor from further non-paid child care.

Not too long afterwards, Mantley went to New York and tried out for a live television program, where he had an encounter with the man running the tryouts. As Mantley explains it:

"Well, where's your picture? I haven't got your picture."...I came up and showed him, *"That's* my picture." "That looks like somebody who's 6'4" and weighs 260 lbs." "It tells you on the back—5'9", 135 lbs." Mantley got the part.

Jerry took pictures of the plays while they were performed and then sold the pictures to the young actors and actresses to use for publicity purposes. His photographs helped his clients get parts.

From 1943, while still employed at the shipyards, he worked out an agreement with the playhouse. The playhouse hired him because of earlier New York connections with members of the Prickett family. Although the studios fired Jerry, the playhouse kept him. He began photographing not only the main stage presentations, but also shows in all the little theaters as well. Starting in the 1950s, he even did the television workshops. According to records at the playhouse, he photographed over one hundred productions. Afterwards he printed 8-1/2-by-11- inch black and white photographs of the performances. At the top of each picture he put a hand-stenciled description of the play that always included the phrase "A Live Action Photograph of…" And the students bought these photos, sometimes they bought a lot of them, and a whole new group of would-be performers showed up each year.

Students, of course, are not famous for having large sums of money to throw around, but it is not entirely unfair to describe these shots of their performances as a necessity. The incident described by John Mantley shows how much the playhouse graduates needed these photos to help them get jobs. There is also no getting around the personal aspect of buying the pictures. Given the out-sized egos actors often display on the one hand, and given their fears that their work would pass unnoticed on the other, many of them compulsively bought large numbers of Jerry's live-action photographs. And they didn't just buy them in their freshman year.

One actor in particular became the subject of a family story. Raymond Burr went rather overboard on his purchases and ended up owing Jerry a good deal of money. Not having the luxury of a collection agency, if someone ran up an unpaid bill, Jerry could do nothing. In 1951, Burr took off from the Pasadena Playhouse to try his luck in New York. To give the man his due, once he returned to Hollywood, he did remember the debt and paid it. Having struck it rich, first in the Alfred Hitchcock movie *Rear Window* and then in 1957 as Perry Mason on television, he could afford the memory. On my honeymoon, I stumbled across an orchid garden he developed in the Fiji Islands. He graciously left it to that nation after his death. Burr did very well indeed.

Quite rightfully the playhouse developed a set of rules that Jerry needed to follow when photographing their students. The management insisted that Jerry's picture-taking could not interfere with any aspect of the performance or the audience's enjoyment of it. No wandering about and no flash photography.

On his side, Jerry needed to take pictures of the actors and actresses without the audience getting in his way. He and the playhouse reached an agreement that he would work during the week, when they had a smaller audience than on the weekends. In turn they permitted him to use the two seats in the first row, center, of the orchestra section of any play he photographed. On one seat he placed his camera bags, and he occupied the other. From that spot, to cause the least amount of distraction possible, he snapped away without using a flash. In the same spirit, he even timed the sound of the shutter snapping shut to coincide with the actors delivering their lines so that neither they nor the audience really noticed what he did. Sometimes he agreed to let me hold the equipment and occupy that second seat. I saw a fair number of plays that way.

The income that Jerry earned from the playhouse and other assorted photographic projects at various L.A. theaters provided just enough to get by, especially given his desired lifestyle. Unfortunately for him, that modest level of existence began to decline in the middle 1950s because the playhouse went into a decline. On the one hand the two leaders, Brown and Prickett, both died during this period. On the other, the supply of students decreased. In the early 1950s a fair number of them, like Gene Hackman, came to the playhouse financed by the World War II and Korean War vintage G.I. Bill. By 1955 or 1956, those veterans who wanted to go into the theater or the movies were already there, and the next batch of civilian students had to pay their own ever-increasing tuition.

Even more personally upsetting to Jerry, because the playhouse people were his friends, rumors circulated of an embezzlement that put the already cash-strapped place in further jeopardy. While the playhouse did manage to survive, it took several years to stabilize.

Meanwhile its problems had an impact on Jerry because, quite obviously, fewer students meant his income would go down. To make matters worse, at one point a relative of the actor, Jimmy Cagney, wanted to do what Jerry did, only with color photographs.

The playhouse management felt it could not afford to alienate Cagney, so they let this rival photographer operate there. He left after only a few months, either because he became bored or because he did not make enough. Someone with a lot less perceptive than Jerry would have figured out that although this upstart had failed, the next one might not. Jerry needed an alternative.

Twisting Joe McCarthy's Tail

Once again, his good luck held. In 1956 he ended up with $40,000, the equivalent of at least five years' pay at the time. Surprisingly, the United States Army acted as his paymaster. The film Jerry used to take the pictures in the theaters became the source of this newfound wealth.

The money came his way because, at this time, his film solved a problem. Using it, a photographer could take pictures inside theaters without a flash. Granted, there were ways to make a virtue out of using ordinary film without a flash in a theatrical setting. Take a look at the book called *Ballet*, by one of the most famous photographers of the mid-twentieth century, Alexey Brodovitich, the photo editor of *Harper's Bazaar*. Here he artistically blurred the dancers' images. At times he also intentionally either over- or underexposed them.

Jerry didn't have that luxury. His pictures had to be crystal clear, with no distortion. In order to take these pictures without anything more than stage lighting, he needed to use a film that had much more sensitivity to light than any film then available to the general public. He needed it because without using a flash, the usual ways of compensating for poor light—opening up the lens further and lengthening the time the shutter remained open—would not capture the action on stage with the clarity he needed. With the ordinary film of the day, after those adjustments, the actors' and actresses' movements would have caused a blurred print, just as they did with Brodovitch's ballet dancers.

Until the 1960s, neither Kodak nor any of the smaller film manufacturers marketed a film fast enough, that is to say sensitive enough, to do what Jerry needed. So he invented just such a film for his own use. It is an open question just how someone with only three years of undergraduate work and a year or so of art school acquired the knowledge of chemistry needed to create this light-sensitive film. The one explanation I found does not seem very likely.

In her introduction to Jerry's film collection at UCLA, his widow claims he found the answer early in his career. For some months during the 1930s, she reports, he worked with a professor at M.I.T. Although she never mentioned the professor's name, she did say he invented strobe light photography.

The unnamed professor is almost certainly Harold Edgerton, and he is quite famous in his own right. His stop-action photographs of bullets cutting through apples and playing cards, along with a single drop of milk splashing back into a container, still make regular appearances in books and art shows. Fortunately for me, Edgerton left his papers to M.I.T. For the period from 1930 to 1936, I checked his surviving correspondence, his pocket diaries and address books, his laboratory notes, and his printed articles about film experiments. I couldn't find even a single note that Edgerton ever experimented with high-speed film or had any interest in doing so. If there was a reference to Jerry in any of this material, I could not find it. I did find, in contrast to Brodovitch's dancers, a marvelously clear picture of a leaping ballerina, but an ultra-high-speed flash, not high-speed film, made the picture possible.

Wherever Jerry found his technique, he did ultimately decide others would want the fast film it produced. Even before going to work exclusively for the Pasadena Playhouse, Jerry had looked at the potential for this market and he needed to find a way to break into it. He also knew that if he found that way, he wouldn't be able to handle all aspects of the business. That is why when my father reached L.A., Jerry asked him if he would become his partner in this venture of trying to market what they called SuperTomic film. Dad agreed to the arrangement and took over the bookkeeping side of the firm, such as it was.

For several years Jerry tried to find a commercial outlet for this product and had absolutely no success. Several factors most likely contributed to his failure. Film wholesalers often had exclusive marketing arrangements with Kodak, or, if they didn't, they feared offending Kodak by offering an alterative.

Another problem was SuperTomic's starting point. Jerry secretly made it by altering Kodak film. If the new film proved successful, Kodak could sue everyone, including the wholesalers. And if the suit proved unsuccessful, it would cost a fortune to defend against it. Those fears had some substance. My grandfather, George, had firsthand experience with how legally aggressive Kodak could be.

When he advertised his film developing at the drugstore and used their name without permission, they threatened him with a lawsuit.

After three or four years of trying to sell SuperTomic to the general public, it began to look like Kodak made the right decision not to mass-market a similar product. But Jerry did not give up. If the film had no wide commercial possibilities, then some branch of government became the next obvious choice. And which branch or branches would want a film that did not need any kind of artificial lighting? The FBI and the CIA do come to mind. If they occurred to Jerry, he never said so. Even if they did, it's pretty easy to figure out the reasons why a former member of the Communist Party might have rejected those options. Nonetheless, he took a rather unexpected route to a government contract.

I know newspapers and magazines of the period sometimes showed aerial pictures taken during the recent wars. They also showed shots from weather balloons. With those facts in mind, Jerry discovered a facility in the desert north of L.A. called China Lake. Starting in 1943, the Navy operated it, sending its planes on practice bombing runs over its dried-up lake bed. Gradually a research component was added there as well, and people from Cal Tech began to appear there. By the mid-1950s, the place branched out even further and tried to find techniques for modifying the weather and for launching satellites. In 1955, Communist Party connections and all, Jerry received a pass to talk with the China Lake people about his film. Evidently they sent him to the Army.

This promising lead almost vanished when it turned out the Army did not have any interest in black and white film. They wanted color. Totally unphased by their requirements, Jerry told them that if they wanted color, he would give them color. He had one condition; they had to give him some seed money for additional research.

During the summer of 1955, I saw him out by the pool taking his handmade color chart, setting it against the light-colored wall, and photographing it again and again. Ironically, the various shades of red caused him particular problems. He ultimately made those reds do what he wanted them to do because, a year later, the Army gave him the rest of his money on the understanding that he would explain to them how the process worked to produce the film, and that he would no longer attempt to market it commercially. Jerry had no problem with either provision.

Looking back on it now, I don't know which part of this deal is more amazing. For starters, only a year before contract negotiations began, the junior senator from Wisconsin, Joseph McCarthy, devoted a great deal of energy to uncovering the nest of communist sympathizers he claimed lurked within the Army's ranks. I can only presume that no one in the Army connected with Jerry's project ever considered the consequences if it came to the senator's attention. In this case, the Army was as lucky as Jerry. They had a contract with a communist, one who had not cooperated with the House Un-American Activities Committee and whose sister had been fired from the Air Force as a security risk. Even worse, they had contracted with this communist to do secret work. It takes little imagination to see the flashbulbs flashing and to hear the wires humming as a smirking McCarthy presented his findings to the nation—the thoroughly disloyal United States Army paid a card-carrying member of the Communist Party to develop a super-secret film supposedly for use against the Red Menace. Of course the senator would claim it actually went to agents of that menace, with U.S. taxpayers footing the bill.

About the only explanation I can offer is that, although J. Edgar Hoover still prowled the nation looking for Soviet infiltrators, and the House Un-American Activities Committee still tried to expose communists in all walks of life, the grip of the anti-communist hysteria had loosened ever so slightly. By the end of 1954, with the United States Senate's censure of McCarthy, it loosened even more. Before 1957 ended, the senator was dead. Jerry always seemed to have good luck when he needed it most.

Sailing Away from Karl Marx

Perhaps anticipating very good luck from some quarter, as early as 1955, Jerry bought the *Anthea*, an eight-meter sailboat he imported from England, and docked it in L.A. harbor. He had been interested in sailing since boyhood. I have pictures of a sailing canoe that he and his friends used on the East River, of all places.

In her introduction to Jerry's film collection, his second wife states that, while working at one of the East Coast shipyards during World War II, he won a scholarship to Johns Hopkins University. There he took what she describes as a crash course in naval architecture. Despite the lack of any commentary by the FBI or

Jerry's draft board, given the way he spent his time in the late 1950s and 1960s, the story may well be true.

To begin with his "new" boat, it wasn't new at all. It required more than a little skill in refitting to make it go fast. Even its lovely black hull that caused no problems in foggy old England, caused a few in sunny L.A. The hull retained the heat and then swelled, causing the deck caulking to pop out. When it did, the boat leaked. I spent more than a few hours re-caulking that deck. Once Jerry did some work on this and other problems, the craft proved very fast. With Jerry at the helm, it won more than a few races.

He sold the *Anthea* for a bit of a profit a year later and used that cash along with his share of the money from the Army contract to clear some of his debts, as well as to buy a tiny house in what was then an unfashionable part of Costa Mesa. He also rented an office in nearby Newport Beach, where he established a yacht brokerage. During his time in New York, he had had a fondest for John Alden–designed sailboats. Now he negotiated a franchise arrangement with them for his Newport office and began his new career as their exclusive dealer in Southern California.

He may have been doing what he wanted to do at that time in his life, but as usual, it had its challenges. Newport Beach did not suffer from a lack of yacht brokers. Jerry soon found he had the added problem that John Alden boats were not well known on the West Coast. No doubt he had so little trouble signing a franchise agreement with that firm, because no other West Coast dealer wanted to start from scratch marketing an unknown brand. In order to survive, Jerry had to branch out. He sold used boats, and, more distressingly for sailboat purists, the occasional motor boat as well. Particularly as the Pasadena Playhouse work slowly dried up, he watched his cash reserves gradually evaporate while he tried to find customers for his sailboats. True to form once again, he managed to find a lifesaver, this time in the form of a wealthy wife.

Safe at Anchor

Back in 1949, in spite of what happened with Mildred and Milton, I don't think Jerry started his new bachelor life with the idea of following Petruchio's example and coming to wive it wealthfully. At first he behaved like most divorced men. He threw himself into the singles game in hopes of getting something other than money from the women he dated.

When I arrived at his Hollywood Boulevard house, at least two of these women occupied his attention, one named Jenny and the other named Charlotte. Both were stunningly attractive, but in different ways. Jenny was tall and shapely, with long blonde hair and a bit of an overbite. She had an English accent, which she came by honestly as a fairly recent immigrant to the United States. She had great enthusiasm for Bobby Short and indeed showed marvelous enthusiasm for just about every project she undertook.

Charlotte, on the other hand, was her exact opposite: a statuesque, short-haired brunette, the epitome of cool before the term became overused. She frequently appeared at the house in the company of her mother. Aside from the mother's hair having a few dignified streaks of gray, they could have passed for sisters. At age nine, I couldn't figure out what Jerry did about the seemingly ever-present mother; but at age nine, I lacked imagination.

With the end of 1951, Jenny, Charlotte, and Charlotte's mother disappeared and a variety of other women came and went in rapid succession. One I remember had the stage name of Voluptua. She introduced late night romantic movies on a local television station. Her appearance pretty much matched her name. I saw her as a kind of made-for-television version of Marilyn Monroe. For reasons that were never quite clear to me, my first encounter with her took place when I came down to breakfast one morning and found she had ended up spending the night on our living room couch.

By 1953, the pattern changed. This is when Anita appeared. Originally she came from a very wealthy New Jersey family that lost virtually all of its money, first through her mother's spendthrift ways, the remainder through the Crash of 1929. Anita went to L.A. not to recoup her fortune, but rather, along with Johnny Weissmuller and Buster Crabbe, to swim in the 1932 Olympics. Even though she didn't win a medal, or come away with a movie contract, she liked the place well enough to stay. It looked like her fortunes revived when she married a reasonably well-to-do man, and they bought a marvelous old Victorian house overlooking Silver Lake. A couple of years after World War II ended, they adopted first one and then a second daughter. Not long afterwards, they divorced.

Although Anita still occupied that lovely house when she met Jerry, I would not call her wealthy. Yet, at first, some money must have remained, because she did not need to work full time in order to live comfortably. Perhaps alimony and child support, which evidently the ex-husband then paid regularly, provided enough for her to manage. Perhaps the family fortune was not entirely exhausted.

Anita's face and form rather reminded me of the fifth grade teacher I disliked so much, but her personality put her in an entirely superior category of human being. As her younger daughter put it, "Mom, you're pretty inside." Anita was well educated, well read, had a quick mind and an equally quick wit. She also knew how to tell a story, a quality I always found appealing.

After meeting Anita, Jerry began splitting his time pretty evenly between her place and ours. Beyond that, for a couple of weeks during the summers, he rented a house with her and the girls on Balboa Island, very near to Newport Bay. From that first summer, I managed to talk my way down there for a couple of days, and Jerry started teaching me to sail.

I think pretty much everyone in the family expected Jerry to marry Anita. He did ask her, but money came into the picture, or, better said, the potential lack of it. In 1953 and 1954, Jerry could barely afford to support himself, never mind a wife. Anita knew that; she also knew that if she married, the alimony would stop. I think that is why she said no to Jerry. Yet "no" is too strong; "not right now" better describes the situation. Five or six years later Anita did need a steady job and began to work as a receptionist at a Jewish center not too far from us in the San Fernando Valley. Perhaps if she had needed to do so earlier, things would have worked out better between them.

Jerry's move to Costa Mesa in 1956 spelled the end of their relationship. If nothing else, it meant their time together became quite limited. Jerry needed to spend his days at the yacht brokerage, and, when a client wanted to close a sale, sometimes his nights. However fitfully, he also still worked other evenings at the Pasadena Playhouse. The distance between Costa Mesa and Silver Lake was great enough that they rarely saw each other during the week.

I'm not sure exactly when Zelda appeared in Jerry's life, but the end of 1956 seems likely. In June of 1957, he announced their engagement to the family. By the end of July, they married in her waterfront home as fleets of sailboats glided by the living room picture window.

Zelda was a widow with three boys. Her first husband's death had left her and her sons quite well off. He had invented a kind of rubberized stripping to use around the edge of the slips where people docked their boats, and then he set up a business to market the product. After several years he sold the business, made a tidy fortune, and bought that waterfront house on Lido Isle, directly across from Balboa Island where Jerry and Anita once had their two-week summer rental house.

In terms of appearance, Zelda favored a page-boy style haircut for her jet black hair. Her features were a bit more rounded than Anita's, and clearly, while Zelda had never been an athlete, they were built along the same lines. Zelda struck me as neither ugly nor particularly attractive. On the intellectual side, she was the only one of Jerry's women to have a college degree. Also, of all the women with whom Jerry associated, she was the only one who had gone to temple regularly. She and her husband were traditional enough or devout enough to have had the eldest of three of their boys go through a bar mitzah

Both of these features, the college education and religious background, caught my mother's attention right away. For the next couple of years, in a whole variety of ways, she would bring them to my attention. Real competition for her had materialized. In the end, the relationship between the two women deteriorated. Some years after Jerry's death, they finally had a big blow-up over a mahjong game, and they never again spoke to each other.

For myself, I always found Zelda hospitable, able to hold up her end of the conversation, and aware of the world. She even gave me advice on the first short story I ever tried to write.

About ten years after I first met her, she did something I thought was particularly admirable. Her eldest son had moved to northern California and had begun living with a young woman he met there. Living together in the middle 1960s was not considered proper behavior for a boy and a girl of any faith, let alone nice Jewish ones. I was at Jerry and Zelda's house with a mob of family when the two "sinners" put in an unexpected appearance.

"Everyone," Zelda called out, "I'd like you to meet my daughter."

As for Jerry, from the point of his second marriage onward, he had no more money worries. Perhaps as a consequence, his life did not change very much. He continued his involvement with sailboats, but the great schemes, the bursts of creativity drifted away.

Despite their adequate income, presumably he and Zelda felt he needed a job, not just a hobby. So in 1961 he came back to his ship design training and the West Coast branch of his old employer, Todd Shipyards. He did fine there for about six months until Todd received a contract from the Navy to build a guided missile frigate. Jerry needed security clearance for that work and he did not get it. Since the shipyard had no civilian assignment for him, they let him go.

For a couple of people with pacifist inclinations, between Jerry and my mother, they nonetheless managed to get on the payroll, however briefly, of all three branches of the armed services. This time, Jerry actually went down to the local FBI office to protest, pointing out that his activity with the Communist Party had ended long ago. It did him no good.

From 1967 on, having moved to the mid-west and visiting L.A. only every year or so, I did not see much of Jerry. On the rare occasions the two of us found ourselves in the same room, we generally managed to get into a good-natured argument over something. In 1977, Jerry died of a heart attack, and I've missed him ever since.

EIGHT

The Doctor and the Lawyer

Building a Cage

During and after my teenage years, family values inevitably made an impression on me. Both my parents, and most of the rest of the family for that matter, believed that only one path could lead to a successful, contented life. The joke about the five-year-old lawyer and the three-year-old doctor was no joke to them. Entering those professions meant success. Equally as important, it meant recognition of that success by friends and family. It was the human equivalent of throwing a family dinner that was beyond reproach. As an extra bonus, achieving financial success in one of two chosen professions automatically led to both social success and personal happiness. At least, that's how they saw it.

Whatever social pressures might have been involved, my mother's view on these subjects came largely from her own experience. As the child of poor immigrants who lived through the Depression of the 1930s, she knew how lack of success looked. Her starting position in the bottom half of society also meant she had an outsider's view of a posh world she could only just glimpse. That's why this image of success and the path she believed led to it had so much power for her. My father had a different starting point, but he, too, felt the frustration of never climbing as high as he hoped to climb.

As I neared college age, mother became more and more determined that I absorb her vision of my future. Her son would be a successful Jewish lawyer. Both *lawyer* and *Jewish* were equally important to her.

It wasn't just some old myth that pushed my mother to have these goals for my brother and for me. Especially in the 1950s, before her reinstatement, she had some rough years. In 1956, my father's thoroughly unpleasant boss fired him. He accused dad of going to the IRS and reporting tax evasion in order to collect a reward. The charge had no more truth to it than the one against my mother, but truth made no difference in either case. Between 1956 and 1958, my high school years, dad worked only in fits and starts. Had it not been for the money from that Army contract that Jerry shared with my father as his partner, it would have been very rough indeed.

Not unreasonably, my mother reached the conclusion that, if she wanted to leave a mark on the world, one that filled her with genuine pride, it would have to be through her children's achievements, not her own and not her husband's. No, if she had her way, she would see to it that I did better than either she or dad. In her mind it was the only way to vindicate all of the sacrifices she'd made. By whatever means, I had to cooperate, to use one of her favorite words. Right through junior high, my attitude toward school was entirely too casual for her tastes. To her it looked like I was leaning toward Jerry's example.

Best Beware my Sting

Her concern did have some foundation to it. In 1954/55, during my final year in what was then called North Hollywood Junior High School, I had an elective to get out of the way, so I took a beginning acting class. In the end, it was one of my favorite classes. It didn't start out that way. Since the skirt-clad performance that had caught the attention of the Long Island newspapers, I hadn't done any acting. At first I felt none too sure of myself. Even though the teacher started us off slowly, just saying a couple of lines in front of the class, when I got up there, I stammered a bit. Right afterwards the thought did pass through my mind that this wasn't the time to demonstrate that I was my father's son.

Things improved. For our next assignment, we had to tell a two-minute fairytale. I chose Snow White. When it came time to have the wicked stepmother ask the magic mirror who was the fairest one of all, I walked up to a portrait of George Washington that hung in the classroom and asked the question looking at him. The class found that bit of business amusing, and so did the teacher. I think as a result, she cast me as Petruchio in a scene from *Taming of the Shrew*, the one in which he first meets Katharina.

Since I knew musicals better than other forms of theater, I thought about using a song or two from Cole Porter's *Kiss Me, Kate* to take back to its parent play. Perhaps I could begin the scene with the song, "I've come to wive it wealthfully in Padua." Two over-lapping difficulties defeated that plan. First, I couldn't carry a tune, which led to the second, looking convincing while lip-syncing to Alfred Drake's baritone voice. After a little experimentation, I realized that the song became funny for all the wrong reasons. After all, I had just turned fourteen and only recently had come down from the alto to the tenor range.

Leaving behind these flights of fancy, I returned to the play as Shakespeare wrote it. In that scene in which the teacher cast me, at one point Katharina slaps Petruchio. In my junior high school they frowned upon students slapping one another, even in a play. So the teacher had us turn in profile to the audience, and directed the actress playing Katharina to aim the slap at the upstage side of my face. The teacher told me that, just as her hand neared its target, I should bring up my upstage hand, and let her hit it. It took some practice, but when done right, that bit of business did make a resounding noise that I rather enjoyed.

One afternoon at home I wanted to rehearse, and when Jerry arrived, I asked him to feed me Katharina's lines. When we reached the line after the slap—"I swear I'll cuff you if you strike again"—I turned my back and tried pouting in an aristocratic kind of way, as though the whole thing fell beneath my dignity. Jerry said, "No, listen to what he's saying."

He suggested that I grab her by the arm, pull her face close to mine, and then deliver the post-slap line. That way, when Katharina responds by saying, "So may you lose your arms," she could then energetically break my grip. Grabbing her would reinforce both her line and her action. It worked for me, and I decided to try it at our next rehearsal.

As it turned out, things backed up in the class. The actors before us were doing the play within a play from *A Midsummer Night's Dream,* and they couldn't get it right. At one point the actor playing the lion screamed and the actress playing Thisbe growled. By the time the teacher called us, she was in a rush, and I didn't have a chance to go over the new bit of business with my partner in the scene. I did manage to tell her in a whisper that I wanted to put in something new, and as we stepped on stage, in similarly hushed tones, she agreed to let me try.

This proved one of our better days, and we both got into our parts enthusiastically and developed a good rhythm with the dialog. When the slap came, despite the fact that the girl playing Katharina stood just over five feet tall, she put some force into the blow, which glanced off my hand and caught my cheek.

"Did I hurt you?" she asked under her breath, sounding slightly worried. Trying not to break the rhythm we had, I didn't reply, but, looking as fierce as possible, grabbed her arm and yanked her right up into my face. Before I could deliver my line, she pulled free, and ran across the stage, crying out loudly, "I didn't mean it; I didn't mean it. I'm sorry if I hurt you!" Once again the class roared with laughter. The teacher just shook her head. It wasn't her day.

By the way, a girl named Paula Robison played Katharina. While she did not go on to become a stage or movie star, she made something of a reputation for herself as a musician. Paula played the flute and I still have one of her albums. David and Naomi Robison of House Un-American Activities fame were her parents.

Perfection

While I had a good time on stage, an interest in acting was just one indication to my mother that I lacked her standards. Another indication was my grades. She bore down on me, especially at report card time, fearing that I would prove a disappointment yet again. My last year in junior high, I walked into the house all excited about a report card with all "A"s in academic subjects and a "C" in typing. Mother's reaction?

"Too bad about that 'C' ruining your report card."

Unless I performed to her expectations in all areas she valued, in no uncertain terms I heard about how disappointed that made her and how in the process my lack of achievement let "everyone" down.

Jews have a long tradition of trying to use guilt to manipulate other family members, and mother showed herself a staunch believer in that technique. Yet I didn't miss the obvious. The "everyone" I had let down was her. Perhaps that's why, after getting worked over on a fairly regular basis, suppressed anger, not guilt, best described my feelings. Which is not to say I then threw myself into acting and ignored the academic subjects. Some of them, especially history and politics, had great attractions for me. What's more, at that point, I pretty much accepted the idea that I would be the family's future lawyer. As far as I was concerned, being a successful trial lawyer and a good actor were not that far apart. I watched Raymond Burr play Perry Mason every week, just like everyone else.

The next few years of my life might well have been a good deal happier if I had realized that any success that came my way would never make up for mother's frustration at not having done the deeds herself. I think it surprised her some that living through her children didn't feel as satisfying as she presumed it would, even when they followed the path she wanted them to follow.

Whatever my problems with mother, no one should draw the conclusion that she gave me or anyone else a hard time because she consciously sought some kind of twisted revenge for her fate. The term *sadist* does not fit her. Sadism implies planned cruelty, or at least pleasure in inflicting pain. While she is the only one who knew what she felt, I'm reasonably sure mother rarely stopped to consider why she did or said something. If it felt right to her, she took action or said what was on her mind; she seldom thought about it much before or at all afterwards. Obviously she did not share the L.A. fondness for psychoanalysis. Still, from my perspective, that personality trait produced inescapable results. The harder she pushed, the more this hidden part of her became unhappy, regardless of how high I flew.

Her unhappiness did not always result in angry outbursts. Sometimes it surfaced as a kind of masked hostility. Not surprisingly, one of the major arenas where these events played out involved food. On many occasions mother would give me a long list of possible selections for a meal and ask me to choose the ones I wanted. Then, when it came time to eat, she and Nettie would present me with something totally different, often something they knew I didn't like. If I protested, she responded, "But we made this specially for you."

Let a Woman in Your Life

From 1956 through 1958, I attended Hollywood High. I traveled over the hills to Hollywood largely because of the way the school-age population spread between the San Fernando Valley and the older parts of L.A. As a result, the school district added a Hollywood High bus route along a thin strip of valley territory containing several hundred students. Of course, eventually the term *bussing* took on all kinds of racial overtones. In 1956, in that part of the world, about the only change in the ethnic balance this bussing caused was to add a few more Jews to the very white, very Gentile student population of Hollywood High.

Newly entering students, of course, occupied the bottom rung of the social ladder. Yet going to high school did not frighten me the way going into junior high had, because junior high worked out pretty well. Beyond the acting accomplishments, starting in the eighth grade, my grades began to earn me the reputation as one of the brighter students.

Starting in junior high and extending into high school, I found a group of other students with whom I had common ground. A boy who lived on the next block named George became my best friend. He was then a tall, lanky redhead who had sharp powers of observation and a great sense of humor. Besides taking the same bus, we began to hang out with one another during lunch time. Along with all his other qualities, George impressed everyone as outgoing and bright. So, thanks largely to him, other freshmen quickly joined our group, including a girl from our bus stop. She had gone to Rio Vista along with George and me, but I lost track of her in junior high school. Now she waited at the same bus stop that I did, and we struck up a conversation.

After getting off the bus in the afternoon, the two of us deeply engrossed in some debate or other, we occasionally showed up at my house to have a snack and continue our discussion. This girl from the bus stop suited mother very nicely indeed. In her view the girl and her family were the equivalent of a royal flush, unbeatable. Besides being Jewish, she was the daughter of not one, but two, lawyers.

While the double lawyers' daughter and I may have had some things in common, she made it quite clear that I did not have the credentials to become her boyfriend. Very early on, she set her sights on someone else, a boy who became one of the class leaders in student government. To be honest, although the girl struck me as by no means unattractive or dull, something about her said, "be careful." I think her tendency to use the privilege of her class status to get her way set off some alarm bells.

While my mother may have lacked sadistic tendencies, I had a few. I do confess that I took some pleasure in periodically bringing this girl home and tormenting my mother with the prospect of a dream that never would come true.

Back at Hollywood High, the double lawyers' daughter became increasingly obsessed with her hunt for that special boyfriend. As a direct result, she let me know that she found conversation with me at lunch unacceptable. I might scare off the bigger fish she had targeted, who was then part of our group.

As it turns out, during this same period of time she became acquainted with a non-Jewish girl who was in several of her classes and who also did not meet her social standards. The solution came to her with little effort; she'd bring her new friend around at lunch time and put the two of us together. That way, in the process, she could get rid of both of us. That's how I met Catherine.

Subtlety was not the double lawyers' daughter's strong point, and she provided great amusement for Catherine and me as she contrived to throw us together. In response we decided we'd pretend to go along with her scheme, but give it what we hoped would be an educational twist for our would-be matchmaker. Catherine and I cooked up a plot to tell the double lawyers' daughter that, after a movie, we began making out, lost control, and had sex. Catherine would then claim she was worried that she might have gotten pregnant, and would blame our matchmaker for her predicament. Like I said, I had a few sadistic tendencies, and, it turned out, so did Catherine.

That next Monday at lunch, neither Catherine nor I could keep a straight face when we first encountered each other. On the way to lunch after one of their joint classes, Catherine told the tale to our target before I arrived. The would-be matchmaker then became quite flustered by that burst of laughter from Catherine and me. Not long afterwards, my bus stop companion found someplace else to eat lunch. In the end, all of her efforts failed to produce the desired reward. That boy she chased found someone else.

I'm reasonably sure these frustrations didn't play a major role in the double lawyers' daughter decision to leave Hollywood High, but leave she did, at least for a year. She took up modeling, and attended a professional high school geared for working students. After graduation, she took courses at a couple of universities at both ends of the state. For a long time, mother clung to her hopes that I would see the light and ask her out. Years later she finally gave up when she heard the object of her desire, but not mine, had married someone else and moved to Israel.

As for Catherine and me, having found at age fourteen that our minds seemed to work along similar devious and iconoclastic paths, we did begin to go out with each other regularly. Why not? Neither religion nor religious background made any difference to either of us. I found Catherine bright, in many respects brighter than I was. She had musical talent and played a couple of instruments. It also did not hurt that she had an interest in acting. As she demonstrated later, especially when it came to the kind of wacky humor of contemporary comedies, she had a good deal of ability in it as well.

Catherine and I dated for a bit over a year. She broke it off. "Cheer up," the old line goes, "things could be worse." I tried cheering up, and sure enough, things got worse.

Panic

In November 1957, George and I agreed to help out with a sports night at the Hollywood High gym. Sports nights featured pretty much what the name implied: volleyball, ping pong, basketball, dancing. It seemed like a good idea for me because it was not the type of event where the students felt obliged to bring a date, and with Catherine gone, I had none. Mostly the evening provided a chance to meet new people without the usual inhibitions of marching from one defined group to another defined group. Sounds great; but about an hour into the evening, I came down with some kind of stomach virus. By the time the sports night ended, I had recovered only slightly.

Unfortunately for me, George, the only one of our group old enough to have a driver's license, had agreed to take home his girlfriend and assorted others. Since he and I lived only a block apart, he planned to drop me off last, and that didn't happen until after his girlfriend had a few of us in for a midnight snack that I could not get down.

Given the way food and family politics mixed together, as a teenager, I looked primed for negative reaction of some kind. This incident set me off. For the next six to eight months, basically until I got my own driver's license (it took me three tries), I suffered from panic attacks. After what happened at the sports night, I feared becoming trapped at a social event. Having to eat at the event, or at least thinking that I did, only intensified the attack.

During that time, I rarely went out at night, and when I did, it took every ounce of willpower to fend off the panic. About half the time I failed. When that happened, I ended up off sitting on the floor in some corner, sweating and swallowing hard, trying to keep from throwing up, and hoping no one would notice. Once I could drive and had more control of my comings and goings, the attacks became much less frequent. Even so, the panic only completely disappeared when I reached my mid-twenties.

All of this sounds quite pathetic, and looking back, it has lost none of its unpleasantness. But a bit to my own surprise, I proved tougher than I thought. Rather than becoming an anti-social loner, I kept searching for ways to pick myself up off that floor. One way involved the swim team. I had joined the high school team in the tenth grade, before the panic attacks began. Once they did, continuing with it seemed to help.

Swimming was yet one more example of Jerry acting as a role model. Jerry taught me to swim properly and to make racing dives and turns. At the time, the Hollywood High swim team was the best in the city and had been for some years. The coach, Ed Warner, was a retread. He started out coaching varsity football. After some problems with the school administration, Coach Warner's superiors reassigned him to junior varsity football in the fall semester and the swim team in the spring. Despite the apparent demotion, he figured out how to develop swimming talent and invented a workout plan that made the skills of already talented swimmers just a bit better.

My contribution that first year proved marginal. I began as a sprinter swimming freestyle and, because the competition became too strong for me, then switched to backstroke. Even here, I always brought up the rear at practices and seldom, if ever, scored among the top three finishers in the swim meets. When I reappeared in the eleventh grade to try out for the team again, Warner told me that I had had my chance the previous year, and now he needed to give someone else an opportunity.

At that point, wanting to keep contact with the team and not become further isolated, I volunteered to act as team manager. The request surprised Warner, but he agreed to it. Virtually no one wanted the job because the work involved doing the annoying little chores such as hauling towels, distributing and collecting swim boards at practices, and occasionally timing the meets. Yet the position did have some pluses for me. During the first year, while waiting for the practices to finish at the YMCA, when I distributed the towels and collected the equipment, I became pretty good at ping-pong.

Gradually, managing came to include more than just equipment. By the fall term of my senior year, with Warner looking after the junior varsity football team, I became the unofficial assistant coach. I ran workouts in the off-season and prepared written evaluations of the swimmers each week so that the real coach could grade them. I even provided a tutoring service in English Literature for a couple of team members who were having trouble and needed a passing grade in order to stay on the team. All my charges passed, so I must have done something right. Doing what I did with them helped me relax a bit and build some self-confidence. That in turn reduced my fear of panic attacks and ultimately the attacks themselves.

My senior year we finally did lose the city championship to Birmingham High, but considering the fact that two of their swimmers went on to win medals in the 1960 Rome Olympics, I guess we had no reason to hang our heads. Actually there is one exception to that statement, the best swimmer on our team. He did very poorly at the championship meet. If he had performed up to his potential, the team would have finished second rather than fourth. Yet, for very personal reasons, his failure did not displease me all that much. Besides the fact that he acted like a stuck-up, unpleasant drunk, the summer before, his father had fired my father after only a couple of months of employment.

Bothering God

In the summer of 1957, when Jerry married Zelda, mother became rather insistent that I apply for a job as a counselor in training with a summer day camp located in North Hollywood Park. The local Jewish center, the one for which Anita worked, ran it.

It is no coincidence that mother pushed this project after Zelda appeared on the family scene. However, her desire to make me more Jewish in my outlook had been there all along. That desire had a variety of sources. The first was the general sense of guilt that she felt about my lack of religious training. True, she decided not to protest when my father became determined that no son of his would suffer through a bar mitzvah. Certainly, by age sixteen, that ceremony had become a dead issue. Yet to mother, the religious knowledge and training remained very much a live one. My dating Catherine probably played a part as well.

Even before I reached age thirteen, in an effort to get some form of religion into our family life, mother insisted all of us try the Unitarian Church. After all, it contained many Jews. Dad had no objections. At that time Pearl and Murray had started attending Unitarian services, and they were the ones who suggested it to mother. I don't think she knew all the reasons this particular church attracted Pearl and Murray. In 1951 its minister, Stephen Fritchman, became an uncooperative witness before the House Committee on Un-American Activities. Because they considered his loyalty suspect, the State Department had refused to issue him a passport. Fritchman was Pearl and Murray's kind of minister.

As it turned out, practical difficulties rather than political or religious ones ended our brief experiment with Unitarianism. Going to the area's only Unitarian church in downtown L.A. meant a long trip from North Hollywood. Getting everyone up and out on a Sunday morning in time for the services required more determination and coordination than mother was prepared to expend at that time. So, after a frustrating few months, we stopped going.

The Jewish day camp was her next effort to make me into the ideal son. During my first year with the camp, it seems to me mother got a good deal of what she wanted. I was exposed to all kinds of Jewish traditions and rituals, and the job required me to participate in some of them. Perhaps because tradition and ritual had never been a part of my life, it made no difference in my outlook. Religious observance still didn't appeal to me. Learning about these rituals and occasionally performing them did nothing to increase their attractiveness.

So, once again, I fell short of what mother had in mind. Using Zelda's family as the model, mother hoped I would lead prayers or at least occasionally participate in ceremonies at home such as Passover. I always told her, if she wanted to pray or conduct ceremonies, I had no problem with watching her do so. After all, I said, when I went to a gentile friend's home for a meal, I had no problem watching them pray.

Mother had another reply in mind. For her, this struggle resembled the one in which she had to convince me to get all "A"s. Only it was worse. That's because once again, to her intense frustration, in the end she needed my cooperation. It mattered not to her if it came willingly or grudgingly; she wanted it. Her way of getting it was to endlessly repeat the request. Some might even call that nagging. The net result? I never cooperated. Zelda one, mother nothing.

As mother grew older, having given up on a formal religious structure for the family as a group, some form of religion became increasingly important to her personally. In later years she told me that she often prayed to God for her children. Actually, what she said was, "I pray for my children to do what I know is good for them."

Wishing Carefully

From mother's perspective, if the day camp did not give me a taste for Jewish ritual, it wasn't a total loss. At least it surrounded me with Jews. I did discover a whole new set of people who happened to be Jewish. All these decades later, I still consider several of them my friends. Many were already adults when I met them. Many taught in the public schools or planned to do so after they graduated college. Talking with them and working with the children at the day camp reinforced my experience tutoring the swimmers. I discovered I could teach. More importantly, I discovered that I liked teaching.

After four summers at the camp, I told mother that I planned to follow my newfound interest by teaching history on the college level. Her response? "I've worked too long and too hard for any son of mine to become a teacher." That is as close to an exact quote as my memory can produce of her reaction to my announcement. For the next couple of days she said that or something very like it many times over and with an increasing sense of betrayal. I'm sure mother never made the connection between the day camp and her newfound sense of disappointment in me.

During my career as a history professor, despite teaching awards, publications with well-known academic presses and the resulting promotions, mother continued to hold those views and, at least once a year, she repeated them: "Tell me honestly, aren't you sorry you never became a lawyer?"

After the summer of 1973, she stopped. I wish I could claim that I cleverly contrived that outcome, but I didn't. That year, for the first time, she and my father came to visit in the town where I taught.

One evening as we went into a restaurant, we encountered two of my students just coming out. With big smiles on their faces they chorused in unison, "Good evening Dr. Schreiber."

I know it seems improbable that it never occurred to mother that the title applied to others besides those in medicine, but until that moment, it quite clearly hadn't. From that date on, but not before, all my birthday cards came addressed to "Dr. Roy Schreiber." It was all right if the doctor was five. I was her son the doctor. And the lawyer? After a varied career, my brother became an FBI agent. All mother's wishes had come true. Well, sort of.

NINE

Full Circle

Political Apprentice

Although a variety of historians try to avoid doing political history, I was never one of them. Politics made an impression on me before girls did. I didn't brag about having a girlfriend until the fourth grade, but at age four, in April 1945, when my father came home and announced that President Roosevelt had died, I understood it mattered. That announcement is one of my earliest memories. The origins of this interest in political life are a bit difficult to pin down. For what it is worth, an acquaintance of mine, one who started his adult life as a gym coach, told me his first memory is of a World Series game. Perhaps our genes control things we've yet to imagine.

In 1948, at age seven, along with the rest of my elementary school, P. S. 134, I knew that Dewey, the Republican, was running for president against Truman, the Democrat. As one might expect in Queens of that era, virtually every student in the school came from a Democratic voting family. In the thuggish, fascistic style of the playground, when one boy foolishly admitted that he (meaning his family) planned to vote for Dewey, a group of us chased him away. Given that view of the political world, listening on the radio to New York City's share of the national results, I got quite a surprise. People, millions of them, voted for Dewey. I could make no sense out of their votes, much less those who voted for Henry Wallace. As a seven-year-old, finding out that elections meant voters might choose even one candidate I didn't favor pretty much pushed my understanding to its limits.

Once we moved to California, my political interests turned into active involvement. The impulse came from within, not based on observing my immediate family. I have no memory of my mother and father talking about politics before we lived in L.A., and then they did so with some reluctance, as a defensive measure. As for Jerry, as I mentioned before, by 1950 his active political days had ended, and he made few comments on the subject unless someone asked him a direct question. Perhaps that is why dad discussed those letters from Lew with me (though still in my teenaged years) before he composed his replies. Of everyone then living in the house, at least I did have a genuine interest in politics.

If the interest itself is indeed genetic, a liberal or a conservative inclination is learned. During the early 1950s, right up through the first year in junior high school, I was as firmly anti-communist as Sylvia. So many years later, the source of these views is now lost. It must have been picked up from some place outside the family, but that is about as far as my detective work takes me. Wherever those ideas originated, I can remember at least one long conversation with a teenaged niece of Sylvia's about reporting all of the communists in the family to some authority. Neither of us had a clue as to which authority. Nonetheless, I'm sure Mr. Hoover and Congressman Velde would have found our chat heartwarming.

As I began to read on my own, as I became better acquainted with the world beyond my family, I started to drift in a more liberal direction. Here the personal side played a role as well. Although I always liked Lew, in California I rarely had any contact with him. Sylvia, on the other hand, appeared all too often for my tastes. I will not deny that my dislike of her played a role in my movement to the left.

Despite my right-wing inclinations at age eleven, I still wanted Stevenson to win the 1952 presidential election. I guess the memory of that Democratically inclined playground in Queens stayed with me. By the 1956 presidential campaign, however, I had moved beyond nostalgia. That contest led me to actively pursue natural inclinations. This particular flurry of activism started just before the election that fall with a political rally for Adlai Stevenson. His campaign held it in one of the L.A. minor league ball parks (the Dodgers, but not their ball park, arrived the following year). Someone at Hollywood High offered me a ride to the rally. When I first arrived, I found that Stevenson looked rather unimpressive in person: short, stout, with a pasty complexion and a thin face.

Even so, the experience of that rally still made quite a strong, positive impression on me. Up until that time, since we did not get a television until 1957, my experience with political activity came through reading newspapers and magazines (most of which, like the *Los Angeles Times* and *Time*, were Republican), listening to the radio, or watching Movietone News before the motion picture started. By looking at what took place in political gatherings at one remove, I lost all of the emotional impact the rallies produced. The people who put together this ball park gathering saw to it that the combination of the visuals, the music, and the fervor of the speakers struck just the right note. To put it more directly, this Stevenson rally drew an emotional response from the crowd. At least as far as this fifteen-year-old could tell, I liked that feeling.

Practical Politics

I'd become pretty idealistic. For me it meant trying to help all people have equal opportunity. That in turn meant civil rights laws that worked. For all this to take place, I also felt that the influence of "big" business on government policymaking needed limiting. Looking at my goals in 1956, not much separated them from Jerry's aims of twenty years earlier. Despite all my idealism, I knew the penalties for picking the more dangerous path to achieving them. Given my family's experiences and my own residual anti-communism, I took the safer route, quite intentionally.

The next step toward becoming involved in political activity came from George. His family had its roots in good, sound Republican stock. I have the vague recollection that his mother might even have had connections to the Daughters of the American Revolution. One day at lunch, not long before the 1956 election, he and I started going back and forth about politics. We ended up challenging each other to get involved with our respective political parties. As it turned out, he had too many other activities for him to follow up on the idea. Especially after Catherine and I parted company that following year, I had plenty of time on my hands.

Someone at Democratic Party headquarters in L.A. referred me to the Woodrow Wilson Young Democrats Club and its club leader, Steve Smith. A bit later I met Steve. He impressed me as someone who looked extraordinarily young for a college graduate. Small, thin, and with smooth, white skin, a rarity for a southern Californian, he appeared rather good-looking in a media-friendly way. Later I found that when he had a particularly pleasing political victory to celebrate, he liked to light up a large cigar. His small size and obvious youth always made me wonder how a cop would react if he saw that lit cigar in his mouth. Steve had ambitions to hold political office, and he started off nicely. By 1959 he became president of the California Young Democrats organization.

In our first conversation, Steve told me quite honestly that the Woodrow Wilson Young Democrats existed largely on paper and provided him with a needed base from which to launch his political career. He had no problem with someone like me joining the club and working to add genuinely active members. The growth of the club could add to his prestige. Just as important from his perspective, as a high school student, I couldn't really challenge him in any way that mattered. About this time another student from North Hollywood High named Eli joined as well. Between the two of us we tried as hard as we could to build up that club and help the Democratic cause. I suppose succeeding in one out of two is not so bad.

In the days before the Internet, political work relied heavily on putting a large number of people on the streets to attract voters. On the purely local level, candidates for everything from the Los Angeles City Council to the California State Legislature, as well as national offices, needed to recruit help from the local clubs. The clubs provided the volunteers to distribute literature, put up signs in public places, and remind voters to go to the polls. They were also not beyond tearing down opponents' signs in the middle of the night. The county organization did act as a central clearinghouse for candidates in need of help, and Eli and I would contact them to see who had the need. The candidates, however, had no way of ensuring that the people would appear or, if they did, that they would stay for the whole campaign.

One local candidate tried the most obvious way of retaining help. Through his campaign manager, he offered to pay me and Eli for our work. The first time this cigar-chomping, overweight gentleman offered us money, we turned him down. The second time, he became quite insistent, and at his suggestion, we agreed to put the money in our club treasury. The perfect compromise—we felt our virtue remained unblemished, and the campaign manager felt he got his money's worth. By the way, the sum involved was ten dollars. With gas at 25 cents per gallon, in those days that was enough to fill the tank a few times.

Notice I keep talking about Eli and myself and no one else. For the whole time I remained active with the club, the two of us pretty much did all the grassroots work. We tried every source we could dream up to build club membership, people who would actually do some of the heavy lifting. Nothing seemed to work for us, including our Jewish contacts.

We did have a couple of frustrating near misses. At one point, for reasons I never entirely understood, a few fraternity boys from USC joined the club. My amazement comes from the story circulating at the time that 95 percent of their student body had Republican sympathies. To avoid the penalties teenagers inflict on members of unpopular groups, the campus Democrats supposedly met in secret, like some communist cell. Perhaps an off-campus club meant less risk of discovery. Of the half-dozen or so students who contacted us and showed up for an informational meeting, only one named Mark seemed genuinely interested. Yet some how or other that interest never quite extended to handing out the literature, distributing signs, or attracting voters.

The Golden State

By the 1960s, California had developed a nationwide reputation for radical politics. It is less well known, but equally true, that in the late 1950s, California was a good place to be young, idealistic, and politically active. The machine-dominated politics of Boston, New York, and Chicago did not act as models for us. California proved too big, too diverse to permit centralized control. Another major barrier to political machines also interfered. Thanks to some early-twentieth-century-legislation at the state level, state and local governments had extensive civil services, with virtually no patronage appointments. Without the ability to reward or punish, political machines don't get built.

As a result, personality, not money and power, played a major role in California politics. Each ambitious political figure, such as Phil Burton from the northern part of the state and Jesse Unruh from the south, had people devoted to their interests. As flattering as that may seem, the real professionals took no satisfaction in this state of affairs. At least one of them from this era described the situation as like dealing with wild birds. Being a wild bird suited me just fine.

As a way to bring some order to this anarchy, in 1952 the party faithful agreed to start an organization called the California Democratic Council. It acted as an umbrella group for all of the clubs and county organizations. Before each primary election, the C.D.C. held a convention to endorse candidates. During the 1950s, the council's influence grew quickly. Only candidates with its endorsement won the primary elections. For the professional politicians this sounds good, but they knew the difference between influence and power. Although Alan Cranston, the first president of the C.D.C., subsequently did become a United States senator, he could not control the groups associated with that organization. In 1958, their endorsement to run for state controller stretched his power to the limit.

Opportunity

As it turned out, when it came to participation in the Woodrow Wilson Young Democrats, the conventions and presumably the possibility of making political connections interested our latest recruit, Mark, the most. For those purposes, he joined at a good time. Starting in 1957, the C.D.C. began planning for a statewide convention in Fresno that would meet in January of 1958.

After some discussion, not all of it pleasant, Steve Smith and I ended up as delegates to that convention, and Mark became the alternate. Although I was willing to trade badges with him periodically so he could split time with me on the convention floor, he decided not to go. I left for Fresno feeling mildly uncomfortable, not so much with the situation involving Mark, as about representing the Woodrow Wilson Young Democrats. Our club roster contained the names of twenty dues-paying members, most of whom I had never seen.

Whatever my personal feelings, it looked like an exciting convention. In 1958 all the statewide offices, from governor to treasurer, required candidates, as did one of the United States Senate seats. For the first time in a long time, we thought we could win. The Republicans had dominated California for the past fifty years. Even during the Roosevelt era, only one Democrat won election as governor, a man named Olsen. He only lasted a single term, long enough to watch the deportation of the state's Japanese Americans at the start of World War II.

Then came Earl Warren. Most of the time, the Republicans proved quite successful in drawing Democratic voters. Through the 1940s and early 1950s, Earl Warren had an especially solid reputation in this area. Yet by the time the C.D.C. convention took place in 1958, it looked like that state of affairs could very well change because of what became known as "The Big Switch."

The switch in question refers to the Republican attempt at having their leading officeholders exchange jobs. It fell into place in late 1957, but it really began as early as 1953. Beginning in that year, the California Republican Party had a problem. Too many of its leaders wanted the 1960 presidential nomination. Then again if Eisenhower didn't run for a second term, the 1956 nomination would have suited them just as well.

In 1953 the sitting governor, Earl Warren, belonged in this group. But after Eisenhower rather reluctantly appointed him Chief Justice of the Supreme Court, Warren's named dropped from the list of presidential contenders. His departure didn't mean the size of the group shrank. Almost immediately the new governor, a Mormon named Goodwin Knight, replaced him. Knight's politics did not match the conservative reputation of his religion. Like Warren, Knight represented the liberal wing of the party. Unlike many Republicans, liberal or conservative, he even had labor union endorsements.

Next in this aspiring California collection, of course, comes Richard Nixon, then Eisenhower's vice president. His triumphs on the House Un-American Activities Committee had paved his way to higher office, and now Nixon had ambitions to take the final step and remove the "vice" from his title, if not from his life. Lastly, the biggest physical presence in this group loomed in the form of Senator William Knowland.

In many ways during the middle 1950s, Senator Knowland looked like the best bet to grab the presidential nomination away from Nixon. It was no great secret that Eisenhower disliked Nixon. That's one of the reasons why the president gave his vice president nasty intraparty jobs like dealing with Joe McCarthy. They did not enhance Nixon's popularity in the party.

On the other hand, Knowland had every advantage. Between 1953 and 1957, he served as the Republican majority leader in the Senate, a post that drew considerable media attention. To add to those advantages, he came from the wealthy newspaper-publishing family that owned the *Oakland Tribune*. In contrast to Warren and Knight, Knowland had carefully cultivated the most conservative elements in the Republican Party. On the foreign policy side, he had a special fondness for flaunting his ties to the ousted Nationalist Chinese dictator, Chiang Kai-shek. Not coincidentally, *Time* magazine publisher Henry Luce found that attitude especially attractive in would-be presidential candidates. Promising as all of this sounds, between 1957 and the 1958 elections, Knowland proceeded to throw away or neutralize every one of his advantages.

Without getting into the question of his basic political instincts or the lack thereof, a good part of the man's problem hinged on his instances on taking the traditional route to the presidential nomination. He wanted to do it from the governor's office. More than a strong inclination to follow custom lay behind his decision. Even after Senator John Kennedy managed to get elected president in 1960, the majority of the twentieth century's successful candidates came from the ranks of governors.

The governors' success at getting the presidential nomination did not come from some kind of statistical fluke. The key to their success hinged upon these men repeatedly getting control of their state's delegation to the nominating convention. They won control far more often than senators, never mind vice presidents. True, because of some unusual and complex considerations, at the 1956 Republican convention Knight had to split control of the delegation with Nixon and Knowland. Most governors did much better, and if Knight managed to stay in the governor's office through 1960, the odds favored him doing so as well.

Before the days of universal presidential primaries or caucuses, control of the state delegation to the national convention mattered a good deal. Even if the state had a primary, victory in it seldom committed the delegates to more than a first ballot vote for the candidate who won the primary. Multiple ballots took place with great frequency because in the non-primary states, for bargaining purposes, the delegations often came to the national convention uncommitted to a serious presidential candidate. Instead, on the first ballot, they voted for what they called a "favorite son."

Granted that the seemingly endless balloting of the Democratic presidential nominating convention of 1920 had become a thing of the past. Yet with the exception of re-nominating a sitting president, first ballot wins remained a gamble. In cases in which no one received a majority on that ballot, the person who controlled the delegates, especially the very numerous California delegates, had many advantages. The stereotypical picture of the party power brokers settling the nomination in a smoke-filled room fits nicely into this era.

With these dazzling prospects before him, Knowland planned on getting control of the whole California delegation by forcing Knight from office, becoming governor himself, and then shutting Nixon completely out of the delegate selection process.

On paper the scheme made sense; its execution, however, did not. The expression *politically suicidal* accurately describes Knowland's actions. Early in 1957, he foolishly gave the game away by blurting out to a reporter that he did not plan on running for the Senate again. At first people speculated publicly and privately about why he decided to leave the Senate. The public speculation often involved the impact of the 1956 election on his role in the Senate. With the new Congress, Lyndon Johnson became the majority leader of the Senate, and Knowland experienced a rather unpleasant demotion to the minority leader's position.

In addition, many people also knew that Mrs. Knowland wanted to leave Washington. Only a very small number of them knew her real motivation. The recent death of Mrs. Knowland's lover, and the continuing affair of the senator with that lover's wife, caused a seething resentment in her that only three thousand miles of separation seemed likely to soothe. Yet when all is said and done, Knowland planned to return to Washington (and his mistress?) as president. He hoped the California governor's office would only act as a two year interlude.

Although Knowland did not make it official that he planned to run for governor until October 1957, his constant campaigning throughout the state for so-called right to work laws that would undermine labor union finances, pretty much removed all doubt about his intentions.

Initially, thinking he could rally union supporters to his cause, Knight tried to make a fight of it. His efforts showed some promise. That's why by late October he received word, through Richard Nixon among others, that if he continued to resist Knowland, he would receive neither money nor newspaper support for his efforts. If he ran for the Senate, however, he would receive both. A month later Knight vanished from the state for a "vacation" and reappeared as a candidate for the Senate. The big switch was on.

By that time many people, including me, figured out that Knowland had targeted the presidency and not the governorship as his final destination. As a Democratic Party activist, I would have worked against either Knight or Knowland. On the other hand, most voters, in all likelihood, would have supported these two very different men if they had run as incumbents. The switch made voters feel used and ignored in the interests of personal power. The Democrats had a real chance to win, if they chose the right candidates.

Picking Winners

When it came to taking on Knowland for the governorship, the California attorney general, Edmund G. "Pat" Brown, had no competition. As far as the vacant Senate seat went, three candidates made it to the C.D.C. convention. Clair Engle, a congressman from the northern part of the state around Red Bluff, became the favorite. A Berkeley political science professor named Peter Odegard and a Los Angeles County Supervisor, Kenneth Hahn, also put themselves forward as candidates. In terms of their political views, Brown and Engle came off as pretty conservative. Brown had been a Republican at one point, and Engle drew Republican votes from his district. Odegard looked like the most liberal of the three, with Hahn somewhere in the middle. I went to the convention in Fresno as a Hahn supporter. I thought his proven, vote-getting power in L.A. would help the Democrats throughout the state, especially since he seemed to enjoy campaigning.

Having decided how I would vote on the major contested office, my next step involved traveling to Fresno and arriving in decent enough shape to be useful. The idea of going to that convention by bus, participating in it, and returning back home again, had me pretty frightened. Despite the driver's license in my wallet, the possibility of panic attacks floated somewhere in my mind. The whole atmosphere of the convention looked just right to bring an attack into full bloom: on my own; no control over my surroundings or my transportation; and plenty of public dining.

At the end of a long bus ride to Fresno, with lots of time to brood, I arrived in something less than great shape. But once I made contact with people I knew and the convention got rolling, the excitement and the atmosphere swept me along. After those first couple of hours, I never had any problem.

The convention took place in a massive, high-ceilinged, downtown facility. Observers and the press could watch from a balcony, but the action involving the delegates happened on the convention floor below. They grouped us by county and seated us on folding chairs. All a delegate needed to do in order to speak to the other delegates was walk up to one of the microphones scattered about the convention floor and ask the chair for recognition. Unlike a famous Democratic convention in Chicago held a decade later, in Fresno no one played games with the microphones by either shutting them off or refusing to give them up to a speaker for a rival candidate. In spite of the tension that naturally comes with making important decisions, the atmosphere proved friendly enough. Even I thought about making a statement on Hahn's behalf.

Several of us from the L.A. area managed to briefly meet with Hahn off the convention floor before the scheduled senate endorsement vote. By that time, he knew he had little chance of winning. His best hope involved either Engle or Odegard failing to get a majority on the first ballot. Then Hahn became the obvious compromise candidate for the next round of voting. It didn't happen that way. The convention endorsed Engle on the first ballot, but his victory came after some heavy-handed procedural maneuvers. The bad taste that left caused a wave of discontent to spread through those of us who had supported the unsuccessful Senate candidates.

At that point, worried about these rumblings, some of the key backers of Brown and Engle decided they needed to do something to calm down the discontent. They tried to convince Odegard to run for lieutenant governor, even though that meant pushing aside two candidates who already had done a considerable amount of campaigning for the office. For reasons I never discovered, Odegard proved difficult to convince. The evidence of his reluctance surfaced when the establishment forces tried to postpone the vote for lieutenant governor. Their efforts failed. The convention moved to an immediate one, and a man named Glenn Anderson won.

While some other endorsements came after lively contests, perhaps the most interesting battle involved a spot way down the ticket for the position of secretary of state. Henry Lopez, a lawyer from the Central Valley area of California, wanted to run for the post. As the name indicates, he was a Mexican American. No other minority candidate tried for statewide office in this election.

A wide variety of party establishment figures deployed their forces to prevent the Lopez nomination. As they saw the politics of the state, the vast majority of voters originally had come to California from the South or Midwest. In their professional opinion, these recent immigrants would never bring themselves to vote for a non-Anglo candidate. As far as the party pros were concerned, a Jew on the ticket in the form of the attorney general candidate, Stanley Mosk, represented about all the diversity California voters would tolerate.

In order to discredit Lopez, the rumor mill began churning out stories, some true, some not. No, we discovered, he had not fled to Mexico to escape a malpractice suit, but yes, he had been married and divorced three times. Even during the convention, that last bit of information did give me some pause. While he did have custody of all his children, I wasn't so sure that fact would compensate for the divorce with the Mexican American and Roman Catholic voters. Adlai Stevenson's divorce did him no good. Not too many years later, Nelson Rockefeller lost the presidential nomination race to Barry Goldwater in large measure because of a divorce. Liberal idealist that I was, I voted for Henry Lopez anyway.

Rumors or no rumors, divorces or no divorces, Lopez won the C.D.C. endorsement and went on to win the primary as well. Unfortunately, in the general election, he went down to defeat, the only Democrat on the ticket that year who lost. I may not have liked the way the party power brokers handled the Lopez endorsement at the convention, but it did turn out they knew who was electable and who was not.

Finding Political Heroes

During that spring of 1958, I had one last political encounter connected with a convention that I remember quite clearly. Once again I acted as a delegate, this time to one of the local nominating conventions held in L.A. After the gathering ended, the Democratic Party scheduled a dinner to which I mistakenly thought I had been invited. I missed the bit on the printed invitation about needing to pay out twenty-five dollars a plate, in advance. The dinner attracted me because of the scheduled keynote speaker, Senator John Kennedy.

At that time I felt the need to find a presidential candidate I could enthusiastically support. On the foreign policy side, the Eisenhower years had left me frustrated. If I had largely left the more extreme vision of anti-communism behind me, I was still very much the nationalist. It seemed to me that the United States suffered a never-ending stream of failures trying to control the Soviet Union. The Hungarian revolt and its suppression by the Soviets in 1956 was the most dramatic example of this failure. Then in 1957, up went Sputnik. Worse, television news showed picture after picture of U.S. efforts to launch satellites crashing to the ground with a burst of flame and wreckage strewn across the launching pad. The failure of those rockets seemed to sum up the Eisenhower years. I wanted a president who could stop the embarrassment, one who could inspire and lead.

After two unsuccessful efforts, I really did not want to back Stevenson for a third try. Hubert Humphrey seemed like a quasi-comical character, with his long-winded and not very elegant speeches filled with wishful thinking and naivete. As far as I was concerned, Lyndon Johnson came across as just as tricky and objectionable as Nixon. That left Kennedy. Before committing myself to doing any work on his behalf, however, I felt I needed to get a closer look at him, even if it wasn't going to take place at the dinner.

As the convention ended, probably to kill time usefully until the rubber chicken dinner appeared on his dinner plate, I heard that Kennedy planned to have a session with minorities in one of the hotel meeting rooms. He probably meant African and Mexican Americans. I decided Jews under twenty-one also qualified. In those days no one worried much about security, so I just walked in and sat down.

I vaguely remembered that after his unsuccessful try for the vice presidency, Kennedy had done some political work in California during the 1956 presidential campaign. What I didn't know at the time was that, during his swing through the state, he had not always made a very good impression. Roger Kent, one of the major figures in northern California politics during the 1950s and beyond, thought Kennedy behaved rather too casually about nearly everything during that trip.

When I walked into the hotel ballroom, I found at least fifty or sixty people in it. Most of them were African Americans, with a scattering of others including the press. Kennedy did strike a rather casual pose, leaning against a table in the front of the room with his arms folded. After some easy questions, an African American man who identified himself as a medical doctor stood up. This gentleman, dressed very well in an expensively tailored suit, spoke with a good deal of authority in his voice. Actually what he said really took the form of a statement rather than a question. He accused Kennedy of supporting a bill currently before the Senate that would bring "socialized medicine" to the United States. In those days such a comment fell just a small step short of accusing someone of communist sympathies.

Okay, here was the test of Kennedy I wanted to see. Reading eyes or body language, I thought the reaction of the audience looked mixed. Surely Kennedy had to know that some of the African Americans there might support the questioner as one of their own, one who had succeeded in a white world. Others might feel, despite what the doctor said, that they needed the legislation because they could not afford to pay for first-class medical care.

Of course on top of all of these considerations, the press carefully watched everything Kennedy did or said. Would he give some kind of vague answer? Would he contrive to change the subject and answer a question that the man had not asked? Would he treat his questioner with condescension in an effort to undermine his authority as a medical doctor?

Kennedy did none of those things. He defended the bill, said it would help poor people get better medical care. Further, he disputed the doctor's claim that the legislation in any way brought the United States closer to socialized medicine. Kennedy ended by saying he felt that doctors in general were entirely too sensitive about the whole issue of the government providing support for adequate health care.

I couldn't vote in 1960 because the voting age was then twenty-one, but from that point on Kennedy became my candidate for president. Even after the Bay of Pigs, the Cuban missile crisis, and the failure to pass civil rights legislation, I still looked upon him as my ideal president. For many years beyond the day of his assassination, I felt that in a second term, he would have convinced Congress to pass the needed legislation, just as Johnson had.

In those years my idealism remained fresh. Granted, I knew that, when Kennedy spoke publically, he mostly used his speechwriters' soaring rhetoric, not his own. I also knew that with his humor, with his public grace in the face of danger—courage, as he defined it—he elevated my spirits and filled me with hope.

That brings me to the point about ten years on where I began this family biography. By then, I'd seen too many presidents and read too many books ever to believe in an ideal one, including Kennedy. Had the politics beyond the Kennedy years remained hopeful, I might have given in to the temptation and tried for an elected office. Especially if I had stayed in California, running for something might have had its attractions. But I didn't stay in California and that's when realism set in. As an atheistic, Jewish, commie-symp professor living in Indiana, any effort to win an elected office would have been a complete waste of time. If I needed a reminder, my encounter with the Hoosier congressman most certainly provided it.

Notes

Cast of Characters

"during its New York run of Gilbert and Sullivan operettas"—Some of these photographs became illustrations in the 1938 book *The Complete Plays of Gilbert and Sullivan,* which has been reprinted several times.

"to paraphrase the Gershwin lyric, are sometime things"—Ira Gershwin, *Porgy and Bess,* "A Woman is a Sometime Thing."

"starving Chinese children when we did not eat our broccoli"—Of course she would have had no way of knowing that the children of Chinese Communist officials received a reminder of all the starving children in the capitalist world when they did not clean their plates. Jung Chang, *Wild Swans* (Anchor/Doubleday, New York: 1991), 246.

"he voted for its candidate, Henry Wallace"—Bureau File 121-42558-20, April 25, 1957.

Success and Failure

"The first year Kodak sold 100,000 of them"—Ian Jeffrey, *Revisions: an Alternative History of Photography* (National Museum of Photography, Film & Television: Bradford, England, 1999), 63, 65.

"The slogan 'You press the button, we do the rest'."—Michel Frizot, *The New History of Photography* (Könemann: Cologne, 1998), 239.

"that device never really attracted large numbers of amateur photographers"—Douglas Collins, *The Story of Kodak* (Harry N. Abrams: New York, 1990), 98-99.

Reds in the Blue

"following him through the pages of FBI files."—While Freedom of Information Requests produced many pages of information, when I requested what the FBI had on the New York City Communist Party in the late 1930s and early 1940s, I received a letter informing me that the FBI had no records for that time and place.

"granted it a tax exemption as a charitable organization."—Walter Goodman, *The Committee* (Farrar, Straus and Giroux: New York, 1968), 177.

"they did get married, by a rabbi. A year later they moved to Los Angeles"—Bureau File 100-22198-14, April 22, 1947.

"the finer points of Karl Marx could produce a lively discussion, if not an intense argument"—Alvin Yudkoff, *A Life of Dance and Dreams—Gene Kelly* (Back Stage Books: New York, 1999), 73, 85; Betsy Blair, *The Memory of All That* (Alfred Knopf: New York, 2003), 16-17.

"they joined a trendy branch of it called the Cultural Section"—Bureau File 100-22198, New York.

"MGM had quite a collection of them, especially among their writers"—Blair, *The Memory of All That*, 202-203.

"well-shot still photographs played a key role in that process"—*New York to Hollywood: The Photography of Karl Stuss*, ed. Barbara Mc Candless et. al. (Amon Carter Museum & University of New Mexico Press: Fort Worth & Albuquerque, 1995), 46.

"to insure continuity between shots"—*The Green Years*, 1946, John Truwe Collection, Academy of Motion Pictures Arts and Sciences Foundation.

"included a shot of Gene Kelly, his wife, Betsy Blair and John Garfield"—Collection 1203, Box 21, folder 5, Special Collections, University of California at Los Angeles.

"he ended up in something called the Hollywood-Miscellaneous section"—Bureau File 100-22198-3 & 10, November 6, 1944 & February 5, 1945.

"rather under that of sympathetic organizations"—John Cogley, *Report on Blacklisting: I. Movies* (Arno Press & New York Times: New York, 1972), 28-29.

"The person is John Howard Lawson (or Jacob Levy, as the agents observing him noted)"—Bureau File 100-21198-17, March 30, 1944.

"only one letter from the Joint Anti-Fascist Refugee Committee to Lawson after Jerry took over as secretary"—*Ibid.*, 106, April 14, 1945.

"an event sponsored by the New York, not the Hollywood, branch of the organization"—*Ibid.*, 292, p. 6, October 23, 1947.

"Meta Reis Rosenberg (producer of the 1950s television show *Maverick*) lived on the same street"—*Communist Activity in the Entertainment Industry: FBI Surveillance Files on Hollywood 1942-1958*, Daniel Leab, editor (Bethesda: University Publications of America Microfilm, 1991) Bureau File 100-138794, Vol. 2, March 4, 1943, 13.

Mr.[?] could not state "what kind of music it was…"—Bureau file 121-42558-7 in 121-HQ-42558.

"caused a good deal of discussion"—*Investigation of Communist Activities in the State of California—Part 7*, Committee on Un-American Activities, House of Representatives Eighty-Third Congress, Second Session, April 20, 1954, 4980 & Bureau File 100-21198-158, p. 10, August 7, 1945.

"out of 319 members, 200 were Jewish"—Leab, *Communist Activity in the Entertainment Industry:* Bureau File 100-138754, Vol. 3, 8.

"He called portions of the movie "a prostitution of historical fact"—Goodman, *The Committee* 199.

"as an addition to the Index"—Bureau File100-335623.

"they should remove his name from the Security Index"—Bureau File 100-335623 & L.A. file 100-22198.

"By 1960, 430,000 files had blossomed"—Ellen Schrecker, *Many Are the Crimes* (Little, Brown: Boston, 1998), 208.

"the bill passed over Truman's veto"—S. J. Whitfield, *The Culture of the Cold War* (Johns Hopkins University Press: Baltimore: 1996, 2nd edition), 49.

"all those in the FBI Deis contacted"—Athan Theoharis & John Stuart Cox, *The Boss* (Temple University Press: Philadelphia, 1988), 176-77.

"He denied the charge"—Bureau File 61-7582-1603, June 2, 1949 in Kenneth O'Reilly, *FBI File on House Un-American Activities* (Scholarly Resources, Wilmington: 1985) Microfilm.

"everything else is laugh"—Stephen Sondheim, *Follies*, "I'm Still Here."

"an early version of the FBI"—*New York to Hollywood*, 47.

"Jerry had not worked in the studios for nearly two years"—Bureau File 100-22198-17, January 13, 1948.

"they moved out of the Beachwood Drive house and in with Mildred's parents"—*Ibid.*

The Wild Blue Yonder

"the petition had circulated two years before my parents left New Jersey"—Bureau File 121-27937, March 2, 1953 & 121-42558 March 12 & 16, 1953.

"in her Air Force procurement division"—Beatrice R. Schreiber File, National Personal Records Center, St. Louis, MO.

"suspended her without pay and finally dismissed her a year later"—Bureau File 121-42558, April 13, 1955.

"no obligation to detail any evidence or explain their actions"—Schrecker, *Many Are The Crimes*, 280, 288, 291.

"Rogers told him, "the moment [had] long since passed"—*Ibid.*, 297

"only if he occupies a sensitive position..."—Bureau File, 121-42558-1, October 31, 1956.

"mother's case was one of thirty-five that needed reinvestigation."—*Ibid.*, 121-42558, December 6, 1956.

"Hoover waited until he received a letter..."—*Ibid.*, 33-9075, April 1, 1957.

"one word about the Air Force request: "Handle"—*Ibid.*, 121-5758-17, April 3, 1957.

"stated that she believes that there was a normal [brother/sister] relationship between the employee and [her brother]..."—*Ibid.*, 121-42558-19, 3.

"The Air Force insisted..."—*Ibid.*, 33-9075, April 1, 1957.

"no recommendation for clearance or disapproval"—*Ibid.*, 121-42558-20, April 25, 1957.

"just a few hundred who got her job back"—David Caute, *The Great Fear* (Simon & Schuster: New York, 1978), 275, 293, 295.

"L. A. Schmuck."—Beatrice R. Schreiber File, National Personnel Records Center, St. Louis, MO.

After Shocks

"If the couple's guilt held up"—Nearly half a century later, researchers in the newly opened Soviet archives found a much stronger case against Julius, but not Ethyl, than anyone in the family knew at the time.

A Pinch of Incense

"information did not make it into his report"—Bureau File 121-5758, March 9, 1953.

"source that gave the information to the FBI (Wheeler)"—Bureau File 100-335623-8, March 20, 1953.

"specific evidence against them…"—Bureau File 62-1664, March 6, 1953 in O'Reilly, *FBI File on House Un-American Activities.*

"also residents of North Hollywood"—Bureau File 100-15732-7, March 13, 1953 in Leab, *Communist Activity in the Entertainment Industry.*

"report on her case from Washington is dated March 17"—Bureau File 121-42558-17, March 17, 1953.

"Hoover has a two word note: "I agree"—Bureau File 61-7582-1531, September 29, 1948, in O'Reilly, *FBI File on House Un-American Activities.*

"Here the note reads: "This is outrageous. We should promptly advise Dept. [of Justice] as case is on appeal"—*Ibid.*, 1630, January 30, 1950.

"friendly…toward the Bureau and its personnel"—*Ibid.*, 1599, May 17. 1949.

"Hoover noted, "I certainly agree"—*Ibid.*, February 4, 1953.

"as I believed there should have been"—*Ibid.*, 1868, February 17, 1953.

"in effect daring the members to do something about it"—Bureau File 100-21198-158, p. 9, August 7, 1945.

"when the Rams played football in L.A."—*Ibid.*, 101, 139.

"getting a committee 'whitewash'"—Bureau File 61-7582-1752, March 30, 1951 in O'Reilly, *FBI File on House Un-American Activities.*

"adjustment than one is aware of in the beginning…"—U.S. MSS 50AN, Box 3, Wisconsin State Historical Society, Madison Wisconsin, cited in Navasky, *Naming Names*, 105-06.

"to talk with Martin Gang"—Navasky, *Naming Names*, 104-05.

"named the members of the committee"—*Ibid.*, p. 85.

"he was not against motherhood"—*Investigation of Communist Activities in the Los Angeles Area—Part 3* (Government Printing Office: Washington, D.C.), 672.

"he planned to attend"—Harold Velde Collection, Folder 94, Velde to De Titta, March 9, 1953, Dirksen Congressional Center, Pekin, Illinois.

"You are excused from your subpena.[sic]…"—*Investigation of Communist Activities in the Los Angeles Area - Part 5* (Government Printing Office: Washington, D.C., 1953), 857-58.

"appeared in executive session before the committee in September, 1953"—*Ibid.*, Part 7, 1954, 4979-4980.

"negatively impact "the national interest"—Navasky, *Naming Names*, ix.

"sensitivity to attacks in the press"—Velde Collection, Folder 94, Velde to Mundt, April 13, 1953, Dirksen Congressional Center.

Making It

"detail about what he wrote"—Bureau File 100-22198-3, November 6, 1944.

"hired him to teach shipyard workers"—Committee on Un-American Activities, *Communist Infiltration of the Hollywood Motion-Picture Industry—Part 10* (Government Printing Office: Washington D. C., 1952), 4496.

"with others on the black list like the director Joseph Losey and Charlie Chaplin"—Howard Koch, *As Time Goes By* (Harcourt Brace Jovanovich: New York, 1979), 206-209.

"renewed Koch's passport after first trying to confiscate it"—Howard Koch, Statement of Political Views, 10, U. S. MSS 50 AN, Box 3, Wisconsin State Historical Society.

"'It tells you on the back, - 5' 9", 135 lbs.'"—Diane Alexander, *Playhouse* (Dorleac-MacLeish: Los Angeles, 1984), 93.

"either over- or underexposed them"—*Ballet: 104 Photographs by Alexey Brodovitch* (J. J. Augustin: New York, 1945) & Jane Livingston, *The New York School Photographs* (Stewart, Tabori & Chang: New York, 1992), 290.

"not high-speed film"—MC25, Series VII, Box 104, Folder 27, M.I.T. Archives

"they let him go"—Bureau File 100-21998-37, March 30, 1965.

Full Circle

"dealing with wild birds"—Frederick Dutton, *Democratic Campaigns and Controversies 1954-1966* (Berkeley: Regional Office of Oral History, University of California Press, 1981), 89.

"split control of delegation with Nixon and Knowland"—Gayle Montgomery & James Johnson, *One Step from the White House* (Berkeley: University of California Press, 1998), 191.

"running for the Senate again"—*Ibid.*, 228-29.

"separation seemed likely to sooth"—*Ibid.*, Chapter 23.

"The big switch was on"—*Ibid.*, Chapter 24 & Roger Kent, *Building the Democratic Party in California, 1954-1966* (Berkeley: Regional Oral History Office, University of California, 1981), 129, 142.

"for a non-Anglo candidate"—Kent, *Building the Democratic Party*, 142-143.

"too casually about nearly everything during that trip"—*Ibid.*, 112-113.